ISTANBUL:

AN ISLAMIC HISTORY GUIDE

ISTANBUL:

AN ISLAMIC HISTORY GUIDE

Dr Muhammad Wajid Akhter

Troubador Publishing Ltd
Unit E2 Airfield Business Park,
Harrison Road, Market Harborough,
Leicestershire. LE16 7UL
Tel: 0116 2792299
Email: books@troubador.co.uk
Web: www.troubador.co.uk

ISBN 978 1805142 720

British Library Cataloguing in Publication Data.
A catalogue record for this book is available from the British Library.

Printed and bound in Great Britain by 4edge Limited
Typeset in 10pt Adobe Jenson Pro by Troubador Publishing Ltd, Leicester, UK

Matador is an imprint of Troubador Publishing Ltd

To my parents

Contents

Why this guidebook is different

"People will forget what you said, they will forget what you did, but they will never forget how you made them feel." Maya Angelou

Today there are more people travelling across the world than ever before. We are experiencing new cultures and locations at a rate that would have been unthinkable a few generations ago. Along with the usual travel accessories, we arm ourselves with as much information as we can about the hotels, the restaurants and the airlines.

We grab guidebooks, more out of a sense of utility rather than to excite any level of interest, because most guidebooks focus on facts, figures and practical tips. While these are useful, they are unable to excite much interest or inspiration in any but the most academic of travellers.

Stories, on the other hand, have a way of sparking imagination and wonder in a way that facts and figures could never do. Stories are used universally, from the cradle to the grave, to get across information that embeds itself in the psyche. It is how humanity communicates what is truly important to us.

Allah chose stories in the Quran as one of the principal vehicles to convey important messages to humanity. This story-telling technique was dismissed by critics as "Asateerul Awaleen" – stories of old. However, the test of time has proven that the stories are still here and still guiding people, whereas the critics are forgotten completely. This is a guidebook of the stories behind each of the chosen locations. My hope is that it will make you *feel* Istanbul and the lessons lying within it in a way that no set of facts ever could.

Why Istanbul?

There are so many reasons to visit Istanbul that the very question as to *why* someone would visit feels redundant. This is a city that is home to an array of different ethnicities including Turks, Arabs, Greeks, Kurds and Armenians. It is a city that has been the Capital of a great Christian and Muslim Empire one after another. It is a city that figuratively connects two different cultures and literally straddles two continents.

Everything about Istanbul speaks to the synergy of these multiple identities. You will find modern hotels and ancient Hammams side by side. You can walk out of a high-tech international symposium and straight into an ancient Mosque. You will see veiled women and tattooed hipsters on the metro, without either looking out of place.

While all these are perfectly good reasons for visiting, there is one reason to visit this city that stands out: Istanbul was the centre of the Muslim world for more than 400 years. It was the last Muslim capital of significance. Walking through its streets and viewing its monuments is like going through the family photo album of Islamic history – full of significant memories and long-gone good times.

In a world where the primacy of the holiest cities is unchallenged, Istanbul bridges the gap between the unassailable holiness of Makkah, the untouchable golden age of Madinah and the more profane and troubled times we live in today. It is a city that brings our recent history to life, and in doing so, it may just inspire us towards a better future.

A Tale of Two Families

The story of Istanbul is one that involves more than a hundred Emperors, perhaps as many ethnicities, thousands of events, but only two dynastic families.

The first dynasty was that of the Byzantines. When the Roman Empire had passed its prime and been riven by splits, Emperor Constantine decided that something drastic had to be done. Usually that meant a change of leadership or possibly trying to gain a newly conquered land. Constantine, however, had other ideas. In a move that still shapes the world we live in today; he moved the capital from Rome to the newly founded city of Constantinople.

Constantine also converted himself and his Empire from paganism to Christianity. No longer was Christianity seen as a heretical Jewish sect on the fringes of society. It was now the official faith of the most powerful empire on Earth. His descendants would rule the Eastern Roman Empire from Constantinople for a thousand years. For most of the millennia, the Muslims were their primary adversaries. Many Muslim dynasties dreamt of taking Constantinople, but only one succeeded; The Ottomans.

The Ottomans were just one of dozens of Turkish tribes that had converted to Islam and turned their wandering, militaristic way of life into becoming the frontiersmen of the Muslim world. They expanded the Muslim world into Eastern Europe and eventually, took the glittering prize of Constantinople. For the next 400 years, the family of Ertugrul and Osman Ghazi became the leaders of Islam and would shape the destiny of the city and the rest of the Muslim world with it.

Why do some families succeed, and others fail? There are many factors involved, but the key is that the House of Constantine and the House of Osman were founded by individuals with a crystal-clear vision of what they wanted to achieve. A vision in the hands of a charismatic leader can be intoxicating. In the hands of a nation and coupled with tenacity, drive and determination – it can change the world forever. Istanbul is proof of that.

A list of important Sultans in Istanbul

Fatih Mehmed II	1444 –1481	Conqueror of Constantinople
Yavus Selim I	1512 –1520	First Ottoman Caliph
Suleyman the Magnificent	1520 –1566	The peak of the Empire
Selim II	1566 –1574	Stayed in the Harem
Ahmed I	1603 –1617	The builder of the Blue Mosque
Murad IV	1623 –1640	Strictly restored authority
Ahmed III	1703 –1730	Inaugurated the Tulip era
Mahmud II	1808 –1839	The modernising Sultan
Abdul Majid I	1839 –1861	The Sultan who built Dolmabahce
Abdul Aziz	1861 –1876	The Sultan who visited Europe
Abdul Hamid II	1876 –1909	The last great Caliph and Sultan
Mehmed Vahideddin	1918 –1922	The last Ottoman Sultan (during WW1)
Abdul Majid II	1922 – 1924	101st Caliph of Islam

Suggested Islamic History Itinerary for Istanbul

Day One (Sultanahmet)

- ☐ Sultanahmet Mosque and Tombs
- ☐ Ayasofya Grand Mosque
- ☐ Topkapi Palace and the chamber of Sacred Relics
- ☐ Murad II Tombs including that of Sultan Abdul Hamid II

Day Two (Eyüp & Edirnekapı

- ☐ Eyüp Sultan Mosque and tomb of Abu Ayyub Al Ansari (R)
- ☐ Edirnekapı Gate of Theodosian Walls
- ☐ Mihrimah Mosque
- ☐ Panorama 1453 Museum

Day Three (Fatih)

- ☐ Suleymaniye Mosque and tomb of Suleyman the magnificent
- ☐ Tomb of Mimar Sinan
- ☐ Fatih Mosque and tomb of Sultan Mehmet Fatih
- ☐ Yavus Selim Mosque
- ☐ Hirke e Sherif Mosque

Day Four (Eminönu & Galata)

- ☐ Eminönu, The Bosphorus, Galata bridge and Yeni Valide Mosque
- ☐ Sirkeci Station
- ☐ Spice Bazar
- ☐ Rustem Pasha Mosque
- ☐ Kılıç Ali Pasha Mosque and Tomb
- ☐ Arab Mosque
- ☐ Galata Tower

Day Five (Besiktas & Bosphorus)

- ☐ Dolmabahçe palace and library
- ☐ Yildiz Palace & Hamidiye Mosque
- ☐ Naval Museum & Hayreddin Barbarossa tomb
- ☐ Ortakoy Mosque
- ☐ 15th July Martyrs bridge

Day Six (Uskudar)

- ☐ Beylerbey Palace
- ☐ 15th July Martyrs bridge
- ☐ Camlica Mosque

Bonus Days

- ☐ Küçük Ayasofya
- ☐ Istanbul Museum of Islamic Civilization
- ☐ Museum of Islamic Art
- ☐ Taksim Square and Pera Palace Hotel
- ☐ Basilica Cistern
- ☐ Molla Zeyrek Mosque

Itinerary

While millions of people travel to Istanbul to visit the city itself, it has also become an aviation hub for many more across the world. This is a welcome change for a city that was once the centre of the world, but time and advances had bypassed them, sometimes literally. Fed up with paying taxes to their perennial enemies, first the Portuguese then the rest of Europe found new ways to circumvent the entire Middle East to get to their spices. Once the route to the Americas and South Asia were charted, so was the economic and military decline of an entire region.

Now, for the first time in generations, things are changing again. With Turkish Airlines operating to more locations than any other airlines in the world and the opening of the massive new Istanbul Airport, the metropolis at the crossroads of two continents once again sits at the crossroads of the entire world.

Istanbul is also one of the most sought-after tourist destinations for the emerging middle class of the Muslim world, who want a place that is exotic, but still familiar. Of course, we cannot discount the pull that Istanbul has in the collective subconscious of the Muslim world. Just as for those from a Judeo-Christian background, all roads lead to Rome, similarly, for 500 years of Islamic history, all roads went to this New Rome.

Here is a proposed itinerary that would cater for varying lengths of stay prioritising areas with the most historical importance for Muslims. There is just so much to see and each area has its own flavour, its own stories, but there is something for everyone in this city. There is too much to pack into one visit, so Istanbul lends itself to repeat bites of the red apple (as the Ottomans referred to it before the conquest.)

The most important thing is not what you see, but how you see it. Will you experience it like a tourist, taking pictures and absorbing only the superficial aesthetic or will you connect with the stories and lessons that echo out from each location? I hope this book will help you do the latter.

SULTANAHMET

1. Sultanahmet Mosque
2. Sultanahmet Tomb
3. Ayasofya Mosque
4. Hippodrome
5. Serpents Column
6. The German Fountain
7. Basilica Cistern
8. Caferaga Madrasah

9. Ibrahim Pasha Palace /
   Islamic Arts Museum
10. Kucuk AyaSofya Mosque
11. Sokullu Pasha Mosque
12. Museum of the history
    of Science & Tech of Islam
13. Selim II Tombs
14. Sultan Ahmed III Fountain
15. Topkapi Palace

16. Cevri Kalfa Sibyan Mektebi
17. Firuz Agha Mosque
18. Sultan Mahmud II &
    AbdulHamid II tombs
19. Koprulu Complex
20. Divan Yolu avenue

Sultanahmet District:

The Reward for Mercy

Allah says in the Quran that "He is the most Merciful of those who show mercy." (Qur'an 12:64)

Before they took Constantinople, the Ottomans came close to complete destruction. A civil war between three candidates for the throne pressed the brakes on their inexorable rise. Eventually, the grandfather of Sultan Mehmet Fatih won, but the whole family and Empire were desperate to prevent such situations arising in the future.

Thus began the terrible Ottoman tradition of fratricide: whenever a Sultan ascended the throne, he ordered for all his close male relatives to be executed. This achieved the desired outcome, with remarkably few civil wars taking place, but at a particularly inhumane price. The funeral cortege of a deceased Sultan would be followed out of the Palace gates by sometimes a dozen smaller coffins of young boys and even toddlers strangled to death so that they could never pose a threat to the new Sultan.

This tradition, initiated by the Conqueror himself, continued unopposed for Sultan after Sultan until it was the turn of a boy called Ahmed. When Ahmed became Sultan, he looked over at his dear younger brother. For some reason, he could not let the weight of tradition negate the bond of brotherhood. Seeing his younger brother congratulate him, but quivering knowing that his fate must be sealed – Ahmed decided he would do something that even the most courageous of Sultans before him had not had the courage to do. He would show mercy.

Ahmed I overturned the tradition of fratricide. A devout and pious young man, he devoted himself to building a grand mosque. He put all his efforts into it as if his time was running out. What he did not realise was how true that was.

Ahmed I died unexpectedly at a young age before his signature mosque was completed. The New Sultan, Mustafa I, would have been quite within his rights to rename the masterpiece mosque as his own. Instead, in an act of true love, Mustafa remembered how his older brother

1

had spared his life: he signed the final accounts for the completion of his brother's Mosque.

Till this day, the mosque and the entire neighbourhood of Sultanahmet serves as a monument not just to Sultan Ahmed; but to the reward of one who shows mercy to others.

Sultanahmet Plaza:

What Did You See First?

This is one of the most iconic mosques in the world. You will have seen it or a representation of it everywhere – from cartoon depictions of the Muslim world to ad campaigns and religious leaflets. It is often known as the Blue Mosque due to the distinctive hue of the Iznik tiles decorating the interior, but its given name is the Sultanahmet Mosque, after its founder, Sultan Ahmed I.

Previous imperial mosques had been financed from war booty, but Sultan Ahmed's brief reign did not see any major conquest. Therefore, to show his contrition in not furthering the lands of Islam, he resolved to make this mosque bigger than any imperial Mosque before it. In this goal he succeeded, but there was disapproval from those who objected to spending lavishly on a gigantic mosque rather than on to the people themselves.

Sultan Ahmed was undeterred. For years, non-Muslims had snidely remarked that the Muslims were incapable of building anything as iconic as the Ayasofya instead, they had to take it by force. Sultan Ahmed and his chief architect – Sedefkar Mehmed Agha – wanted to disprove this once and for all by building a structure so magnificent that the gaze of everyone would be drawn to it before the Ayasofya.

Joseph Campbell once said, "If you want to understand what's most important to a society, don't examine its art or literature, simply look at its biggest buildings" (Campbell, 1988). While there were many other worthy ways that the money could have been spent, investing in the self-confidence and prestige of a people is difficult to put a price tag on.

Even today, as you walk into the main plaza with two of the most beautiful buildings in the world, your gaze is inevitably drawn towards one before the other. The Sultanahmet Mosque is not just an architectural masterpiece, it was also a statement by the Ottomans that they had eclipsed the Byzantines in glory and power – and that their faith would not accept second place to any other.

Sultanahmet Mosque:

The Ghost of Empires Past

The Blue Mosque is located on the site of the Palatium Magnum – the Great Palace of the Byzantine Emperors. For almost 700 years, this was the heart of the Eastern Roman Empire and where the central Government was located. This was the place where plans to divide and disrupt the Muslim world were hatched including supplying and organising the various crusader forces on their way to the Holy Land, stoking the disastrous civil war of Bayezid and Timur and encouraging the Mongol invasion of Muslim heartlands.

By the time Mehmed II conquered the city, the palace was a shell of its former self, largely laying in ruins due to sacking by the crusaders in the fourth Crusade and years of siege and conflict. A few remains of the old palace have been found under the Arasta Bazaar and, after the conquest, new smaller palaces for Ottoman government officials were constructed there. However, all were purchased centuries later so that the Palace of the Byzantine Emperors could give way to the House of Allah, the current Sultanahmet Mosque. Hence what had been the centre of intrigue and scheming, was now the same spot where the adhaan would be called out five times a day.

After conquering Constantinople, Sultan Mehmed Fatih went to visit the famous Palatium Magnum. While wandering through the magnificent, but deserted halls and admiring the monumental designs, he was moved by the melancholy emptiness and is said to have recalled the haunting lines of poetry by the poet Firdausi: "the spider spins his web in the Palace of the Caesars, the owl hoots in the towers of Afrasiyab." (Runciman, 1990)

It is a testament to great people that they rarely are comfortable revelling in their victories and instead are constantly looking ahead to what happens next. At the time of his greatest triumph, instead of hubris, Mehmet Fatih was in a reflective mood. Now at the pinnacle of his power, he was reminding himself that all worldly glory is fleeting, and that only the afterlife is eternal.

The Door to the Sultanahmet Mosque:

A Reminder Who the Real King is

There are always going to be some perks to being royalty. Sometimes this means having the biggest palace in the city and other times it means never having to pay taxes. In the Ottoman Empire, one of the benefits was that only the Sultan could ride into the courtyard of the mosque on his horse.

This was quite a nice perk, but the architects of the Imperial mosques made an adjustment that would ensure that such a perk did not go to the ruler's head, quite literally. The chain that you see hanging in the doorway was installed so that if the Sultan did decide to ride in on his horse, he would have to bend his head down to avoid a collision. This forced bowing was designed to instil humility inside the sovereign when he entered the House of Allah. It reminded him that no matter how great a ruler he was, Allah was greater.

Sultanahmet Minaret:

The Strange Connection to Makkah

For anybody concerned with symmetry, travelling to the Masjid al-Haram, until recent years, would have prompted some consternation; why were there three pairs of minarets and then one minaret on its own? Had they run out of money and been unable to complete a pair? Did they want to keep the number of minarets odd? Was it out of sheer neglect?

The answer lay thousands of miles away in Istanbul.

The legend goes that Sultan Ahmed I had asked the architect of the Blue Mosque to build "altin minaret" (golden minarets), but the architect misheard him and instead made "alti minaret" (six minarets). The construction of six minarets created a commotion in the city as only the Haram in Makkah was allowed that number. The whispers grew louder about the impertinence of the Sultan to dare have his mosque compete with the grand mosque of Makkah. The thought of destroying a minaret once constructed could not happen either as this would be a bad deed.

Sometimes, when stuck between two unpalatable outcomes, it takes quick thinking and creativity to find solutions where others can only see problems. Just when the crisis seemed to be unfixable, Sultan Ahmed came up with an idea that would not involve destroying a minaret or disrespecting the Haram in Makkah. He ordered the construction of a seventh minaret at the Haram and declared that from then on, no other mosque in the world should have that number. So, the next time you look up at the minarets of the Grand Mosque in Makkah or the Blue Mosque in Istanbul, remember how they are connected by the ingenuity of our predecessors.

Muezzin Mehfil:

A complicated relationship with race

The black flag on the muezzin's platform and the calligraphic panel nearby invokes the name of Bilal ibn Rabah (RA): the first muezzin in the history of Islam. This is found in many Ottoman mosques. Bilal (RA) was an iconic figure in Islamic history but unfortunately also one of the most tokenised figures. Although the prominent reverence shown to him in the largest mosque in Istanbul gives the impression that the Ottomans were enlightened in terms of race, the reality was not so rosy.

Like most societies of the time (and currently), race and ethnicity played overwhelming roles in the status and prospects of individuals. Unlike their contemporaries in other Empires, Black Ottomans could be rich and even powerful. For example, the chief Black Eunuch was one of the most senior officials in the Empire; in some eras only superseded by the Sultan and the Valide Sultan.

However, the Ottomans still benefited from a slave system that was racist and dehumanising. Captured Africans were robbed of agency, freedom and often mutilated to allow them to serve in the Harem. This was often done by third parties. Some slaves were Caucasian and sometimes the slaves were treated with genuine kindness that their contemporaries in other Empires would have envied. However, none of this can absolve them from the moral consequences of slavery.

The way that women, Africans, non-Muslims and others were treated in the Empire may have been more enlightened than other contemporary societies, but it still fell short of the Islamic ideals that were given to us in Madinah. Ultimately, a slave dressed in a beautiful kaftan and with important responsibilities was still a slave. Seeing the name of Bilal (R) celebrated in mosques across Istanbul is a reminder of the unifying vision of Islam and the importance of raising standards, not just flags.

Hünkâr Mahfili:

How to Lose Touch and Make Enemies

A house of worship is the last place you would expect to find an exclusive VIP section, but yet, here it is. The Hünkâr Mahfili, or the Emperor's Lodge, was built to allow the royal family to have privacy and safety when attending the daily prayers. It was an unwelcome, but possibly necessary innovation, especially as Muslim rulers had nasty habit of being stabbed to death during prayers. Two out of the first four Rightly Guided Caliphs were assassinated this way. By praying in this protective and often elevated cage, the Ottoman Sultans were much less likely to be assassinated than their predecessors.

The Hünkâr Mahfili in the Blue Mosque also served as the Headquarters of what came to be known as "The Auspicious Incident." This was the day that the Ottoman Empire did what no other force in the world was able to do until that point – destroy the Janissaries.

The Janissaries were the elite fighting force of the Ottomans: think the SAS or Navy Seals, but far more powerful. They were known throughout the world for their skill and ability to turn the tide of any battle they entered. At the outset, their members were all non-Muslim children taken from their families and raised in the home of the Sultan.

Their extreme personal loyalty meant they would do anything to protect him and his Empire. It was also what made them so dangerous. Over the centuries, they realised that they could not only protect the Sultan, but they could control him. They had turned corrupt and out of control. When there were no wars from which they could profit, they would start fires, extort communities and generally terrorise the population. However, as hated as they were, the Janissaries were still too powerful to challenge. Sultan after Sultan was unable to deal with them and a few were even removed or killed by them.

Sultan Mahmud II realised that the only way to get rid of them was a purge that took 18 years to coordinate and execute. Finally in 1826, Sultan Mahmud II sent secret sealed orders to be opened in mosques across Istanbul simultaneously. At that given moment, the purge was signalled when the cloak of the Prophet ﷺ was unfurled on the minbar of the Blue

Mosque. Imagine the scene unfolding before you, the imam holding aloft the cloak of the Prophet ﷺ and demanding the faithful to obey their Caliph and Sultan – hunt down every last Janissary.

By the end of the day, the Janissaries were all dead – many hundreds piled one on top of the other in the Hippodrome. It was the Hünkâr Mahfili of the Sultanahmet Mosque that served as the military Headquarters of the Grand Vizier during the annihilation of the Janissaries in 1826. Their corruption had ended, but the Ottomans had also destroyed their most loyal and effective fighting force, rather than reforming it. The Blue Mosque could go back to being a mosque, but the Empire would never be the same again.

Sedefkar Mehmed Agha:

Sometimes Setbacks are Doorways to Success

Mehmed Agha was a young Albanian who appeared to have voluntarily joined the Ottoman civil service as he had a genuine interest in governance. Fate had other plans. Although initially trained in music and then mother of pearl carpentry (from where he got his title of Sedefkar), he left that field to work in politics. After years of working his way up the career ladder, he finally found himself in the office of the Governor of Damascus as one of his deputies. During his time there, he was given the high honour of leading one of the Hajj caravans when a curious incident occurred that would change his life – and Istanbul's skyline – forever.

During the night, the Hajj caravan was robbed by marauding bedouins. Later that same evening he had a dream in which he was told that he would come across them again and that he should spare none of them. A few hours later, just as his dream had predicted, he stumbled across the same bedouins who had just robbed his Hajj Caravan. They were sound asleep. Acting on his dream – he attacked. By the end of the night every one of them was killed. Sedefkar Mehmed refused to take any prisoners.

While he was initially celebrated for avenging the Hajj caravans, his enemies saw this as their chance to clip his wings and started a campaign against him. They claimed that Sedefkar Mehmed acted recklessly and extra-judicially. It worked and he was eventually demoted from his lofty position to start from scratch in an entirely different department. This would be enough to break most men, but Sedefkar Mehmed Agha was not most men. Thus, at an advanced age, Sedefkar Mehmed Agha found himself restarting his career again as an apprentice architect. His boss? An up-and-coming architect called Sinan.

Sedefkar learnt all he could from his master, but when Sinan eventually died, Sedefkar was passed over for the role of chief architect. Twice. Finally, in his old age and after a lifetime of having multiple careers cut short, Sedefkar Mehmed Agha became the chief architect of the Ottoman Empire. His patron was the newly crowned Sultan Ahmed.

There are often many setbacks in life, but perseverance is the fuel that separates great people from the rest of the pack. Sedefkar Mehmed Agha had this in spades. Instead of being an unknown Governor of some town, Sedefkar Mehmed Agha went on to be the architect and builder of the beautiful Blue Mosque, one of the most iconic buildings in the world.

Sultanahmet Mosque Blue Tiles:

It's What on the Inside that Counts

The Sultanahmet Mosque is more popularly known as the Blue Mosque because of the blue Iznik tiles that cover the *interior* of the mosque. This vibrant blue colour was a firm favourite of the Ottomans – so much so that the French invented a new word to describe this hue: "turquoise" (literally, "of the Turks").

Iznik tiles are not your ordinary mass-produced tiles that you can get in any store. Each tile is a work of art in its own right, with original pieces selling for exorbitant amounts in auctions these days. The construction of the Mosque required so many of these exceptional tiles that the entire city of Iznik could not churn them out fast enough. Sultan Ahmed never did feel like time was on his side and decided to strip the beautiful blue tiles from his own palace to get the job done. This is why, even now, the walls of the Imperial bathrooms are virtually tile free.

The Prophet ﷺ once said, "Verily, Allah does not look at your appearance or wealth, but rather He looks at your hearts and actions." (Sahih Muslim) Islam puts much value on avoiding judging people or objects based on superficial outward appearances. Just like we should not judge the Blue Mosque by its rather plain exterior, but by looking deeper and discovering its dazzling interior, so too applies to many beautiful souls who are around us today.

Sultanahmet Tomb:

Who was Sultan Ahmed?

Although his ancestors included The Conqueror, The Saint and The Magnificent – Sultan Ahmed came to the throne in 1603 at the age of thirteen and showed right from the start that he would do things differently. Up to that point, whenever an Ottoman Sultan came to the throne, all his male relatives would be executed so that there would be no possibility of civil war.

The Ottomans justified this by getting religious scholars to concede that the death of a few was preferable to the potential death of thousands. However, no amount of legal arm twisting could hide the fact that at the end of the day, this was a barbaric practice. Sultan Ahmed had this tradition abolished and as a com- promise, kept his brother under virtual house arrest in the Palace.

Sultan Ahmed was very pious and spent much time and effort in promoting Islamic values in the Empire. It is said that he would patronise the scholars of Islam, encouraged the payment of Zakah, disliked music and paintings of living creatures.

He had a special attachment to the memory of the Prophet (SAW.) Upon his ascension to the throne, he had the largest diamonds in the treasury sent to Madinah and pinned near the grave of the Prophet (SAW.) He placed a tracing of the Prophet ﷺ's foot in his turban to remind himself that honour and power resided in following the Messenger and the commands of Allah.

The greatest evidence of his love of the Prophet ﷺ can still be seen when you go to visit the Prophet ﷺ in Madinah. Next to the Mawajaha Al Sharifa – the Sacred Meeting point – with the viewing hole that corresponds to where the Prophet ﷺ is facing us, there is a large silver plaque where Sultan Ahmed I wrote a message praising the Prophet ﷺ and asking for his intercession on Judgement day.

Although Sultan Ahmed lived for a relatively short period and died before he was even 30 years old, his legacy remains with us, not just in the mosque and district named after him, but also in the passion for his faith that palpably affected his descendants and his people.

Sultanahmet Tomb:

Kosem and True Power

In the Ottoman Empire you kept your enemies close and your children closer. This was a reflection of the inherent flaw within any monarchy: your children and relatives stood to gain dramatically by your demise. It inverts the traditional loyalties within a family and shows how power can corrupt even the most sacred of bonds.

Time after time, sons deposed their own fathers and fathers ordered the execution of their sons. Such barbarity is difficult for us to imagine in a normal context, but power corrupts, and absolute power can corrupt absolutely. The Ottoman Empire was riven with such rivalries, with later Sultans even being deposed by their half-brothers.

The tomb of Sultan Ahmed is a small exception to this unnatural rule. Sultan Ahmed takes the central position here as befits the patriarch and the patron of the building. Around him are two of his children who became Sultans in their own right and then other relatives of lesser political importance.

However, arguably, the most fascinating person buried here is not one of the three Sultans but Kosem Sultan – the favourite of Sultan Ahmed I. One of the most incredible women in the history of Islam, she was able to not just survive in an incredibly patriarchal society, but came to dominate it. She began life as the unknown daughter of a Greek priest and ended it as one of the most powerful women in the world. When the Ottoman Empire reeled from a succession of young or weak-minded rulers, stability was provided by Kosem who ensured that the wheels of state ran smoothly – regardless of who sat on the throne.

She corresponded with other powers including Queen Elizabeth I, she looked after the welfare of the poor through charity and promoted a meritocratic wave of promotions at court. She was the true power in the Empire for many decades and did more than anyone else to keep her family and the Empire together. The Sultans may have sat on the throne, but it was Kosem who ruled.

Hippodrome:
The Original Sports Stadium

The Hippodrome, like its older cousin the Coliseum, was an original sports stadium. Located in the heart of Constantinople, the masses and the elite of the Byzantine Empire would gather here to watch horse races across the track. The venue was also furnished with a large obelisk from Egypt that you can still see a part of today. Capable of holding up to 100,000 people in the stands, the actual venue is older than the Byzantine Empire as it was built by the Roman Emperor Septimius Severus.

There would usually be two teams of horse or chariot racers: the Greens and the Blues. The supporters of each would be fanatical in their loyalty to their side and even wear clothing items of the same colour. Sounds familiar? Just like at modern sporting events, sometimes things would get out of hand and fighting between the different teams would lead to riots.

On at least one occasion, the supporters went further than any modern hooligan could ever dream of. During the reign of the great Justinian, fans from both sides were found to be operating a criminal ring involved in murder. Despite being a passionate Blue team fan, Justinian tried to punish the murderers equally.

As he was watching the game from his balcony next to the Hippodrome, the crowd turned against him and launched a full-on rebellion. One of the most significant Byzantine Emperors, was on the verge of giving up when his wife Theodora rebuked him for his cowardice. By the end of the revolt, the mobs had burnt half the city, killed tens of thousands of people and destroyed the Ayasofya. What had started as a way of distracting the people had transformed them into mindless fanatics that thought only about their team.

Eventually, Justinian regained control and vowed to rebuild back bigger and better. The legacy of that vow lies behind you. It is the wonder of the world that is the Ayasofya today.

The Serpent Column:

Saving the West

After the battle of Thermopylae, the Persians were prevented from taking over the whole of Greece at the battle of Salamis. This is often considered as one of the most critical battles in history, for if the Greeks had lost that day, much that is now the foundation of Western civilization, may have never survived.

The next invasion by the Persians was checked at the battle of Plataea. This battle is not known as much but was no less crucial to ending the threat of Persia on mainland Greece. Although not highly regarded by historians these days, it seems it was a huge deal for the Greeks as they melted down the shields and weapons of the Persians and cast the molten bronze into a column.

The column was of three intertwined snakes representing the 31 different city states that had united together to ward off the powerful Persians. The names of each city state were written on the bodies of the serpents and the entire sculpture was moved to one of the most holy places in all of Greece – the temple of Apollo at Delphi.

The sculpture stayed there till Constantine moved it to his new capital of Constantinople and placed it in a prime location. The golden bowl that sat atop the serpent heads was stolen during the fourth crusade. The heads were smashed off, but there is a lot of discrepancy as to who did it. Some say it was an Ottoman Sultan wanting to show his strength, but others point to a European diplomat keen to take a memento home with him. Either way, the headless column still survives, a monument to the survival of Greek and Western civilization.

The German Fountain:

A Poisoned Gift

What happens when you cross German engineering with Ottoman design? Well, at least one of the answers is this rather garish fountain. At the end of 1800s, Kaiser Wilhelm of Germany was desperate to get the Ottoman Empire, and the Muslim world as a whole, ally with him in an attempt to break the colonial monopoly of the British, Russian and French. Wilhelm felt that if the Ottomans were able to unite the Muslims on the side of the Germans, he would be in a much better position in the coming World War.

Sultan Abdul Hamid II was, quite rightly, keen to avoid getting directly involved on either side and kept playing one side off against the other. Wilhelm was undeterred and did his best to win Muslim favour, even going so far as spreading the rumour that he had converted to Islam and had gone on the Hajj in secret. He personally paid for a new marble tomb to be erected over the grave of Salahuddin Ayyubi and toured more parts of the Ottoman Empire than even the Sultan.

Part of his PR campaign included gifting the fountain in the Hippodrome to the Ottoman people. You will see that the interior of the dome has the tughra of Sultan Abdul Hamid II as well as the Teutonic "W" of Wilhelm.

The charm offensive eventually worked – once Sultan Abdul Hamid II was conveniently removed by the Young Turks. The Ottomans would eventually take part in World War I on the side of Germany and the Axis – a decision that would spell the end of both their Empires. Though it may just seem like a slightly odd-looking fountain in the heart of old Istanbul, it is really a monument to bad choices and a stark lesson; be careful about who your enemies are but be even more careful who you make friends with.

Ibrahim Pasha Palace:

From favourite to executed

This ancient palace that stood in the prime location of the hippodrome was the venue for the meteoric rise and spectacular fall of one the more colourful characters in Ottoman history. Pargali Ibrahim was a son of a Greek sailor who was captured and sold into slavery. He ended up in the Ottoman palace that the young Suleiman the Magnificent was growing up in. They became best friends and when Suleiman became Sultan, he promoted Ibrahim rapidly. It helped that Ibrahim was something of a master of all trades who spoke many languages and was as good in military matters as he was in restructuring the civil service.

Suleiman even married his favourite sister Khadijah to Pargali Ibrahim. But it is impossible to rise so rapidly without making many enemies. Many viziers who felt Ibrahim had taken roles that they had worked hard for, resented him. The common people were suspicious of his "frank" roots, which he did not seem to be particularly ashamed of. Finally, Ibrahim made an enemy of the one person who was closer to Suleiman than even he was – Haseki Sultan Hurrem.

She filled Suleiman's ears against Ibrahim, but he resisted her requests to remove him. However, he was not able to resist them forever. After a campaign in Europe, Ibrahim had three of the statues from the main cathedral brought back and installed right outside the palace. The Muslim population were scandalised, and a poet satirised the incident by saying "Prophet Ibrahim used to break idols, but Pasha Ibrahim installs them." In a fit of anger, Ibrahim had the poet executed.

This was the last straw. Public opinion had decisively turned against the all-powerful Ibrahim. Despite his considerable skills, he had become a liability. Soon after, Ibrahim and Suleiman dined together in the private apartments of the Sultan as they had so often done in the past. The next morning, his strangled body was found outside the palace. An ignominious end to a promising career.

Ibrahim Pasha had gone from Makbul Pasha (the favourite) to Maktul Pasha (the executed) and given us all a salient lesson in the perils of arrogance and complacency.

Turkish and Islamic Arts Museum:

A wealth of treasures

This former palace of Ibrahim Pasha was used as the residence of Grand Viziers. Eventually, after the fall of the Ottoman Empire, it was scheduled to be pulled down and replaced by the Justice Department. However, a passionate article in a newspaper by an eminent historian meant it was – at least partially – preserved. The gallery looking out onto the Hippodrome is the perfect vantage point to enjoy a unique view of the Blue Mosque and the grounds before you, aligning with the obelisk of Thutmose III.

The spacious building served as the perfect location for preserving the beautiful art produced in the Ottoman Empire and before it. Here you will find intricate carpets, manuscripts and thousands of Qurans. Amongst these treasures you will find a prayer rug from the tomb of Alauddin Keykabut – the former Seljuk Sultan of Rum. You will also find old keys to the Kaaba and even a Qibla Numa, which was an instrument similar to an ancient Qibla finder app.

The carpets here are exquisite and for the uninitiated into this particular art, may go, unappreciated. Each carpet here may have easily taken a year of a master craftsman's life or more. They were the ultimate possession that would transform any location into a home. They were handmade and built to last, with a carpet considered brand new for at least 50 years.

Of particular interest to Muslims are the early Quran fragments saved from the Umayyad Mosque – some as early as 876 C.E. or 262 years after Hijra. As Damascus fell to the French and the ragtag militias of the Arab revolt, the Ottomans tried to save some of the most valuable artefacts rather than risk losing them to a French museum. Unfortunately, their German allies had other ideas and carted off many priceless items to Berlin to be stored and displayed in their own museums where they remain to this day.

Küçük Ayasofya:

Saving the life of an Emperor

There are many great Emperors of the Byzantine Empire, but none save Constantine the Great could compare to Justinian. Born into a humble peasant family, the young Justinian benefitted from the meteoric rise of his uncle Justin. Justin was the commander of an Imperial guard unit, who struck it lucky by finding himself in the right place at the right time when he became the Byzantine Emperor after a typically messy succession crisis.

Justin had no children and so adopted his nephew Justinian as his heir. Things were going well with Justinian proving himself an able and quick learner. However, there were enough rumours going around court that Justinian was plotting to remove the aged Justin.

Justinian's uncle, the Emperor Justin I, sentenced him to death for plotting to dethrone him. Justinian's life was spared at the last moment when Justin saw a dream in which the Christian saints, Sergius and Bacchus, appeared absolving his nephew of the crime of attempted regicide.

The ever-grateful Justinian swore to build a magnificent church in their honour. When he became the Byzantine Emperor, he honoured this commitment, and the result was Küçük Ayasofya. Küçük is Turkish for little, and this name was given because this particular building is an obvious forerunner of the much greater Ayasofya to be built next to the royal palace.

Justinian would go on to become one of the greatest Roman Emperors to ever live, even managing to reunite the Empire (even if briefly) by a string of unbroken conquests in Europe and North Africa. There were many parallels between Justinian and Suleiman the Magnificent. Both ruled Istanbul, both built huge places of worship, both married their concubines, both set up new codes of law and both conquered huge swathes of territory. The similarities do not end here. Both were the highpoint of their civilization from which fortunes began to turn.

Eventually, the church was converted into a mosque by the chief Black eunuch of Bayezid II, Hussein Agha. Just like its big sister – the Ayasofya, the Küçük Ayasofya still has traces of its Christian past preserved for no reason other than to avoid needless destruction of the heritage of others. For example, the Baptismal font is still located under the carpets and if you ask the Imam, he may uncover them for you in between prayers.

Caferağa Madrasa:

Everyone is in it for the afterlife

Located next to the Ayasofya mosque, this small madrasa was built by Mimar Sinan on the orders of Cafer Aga – a palace official at the time of Sultan Suleiman the Magnificent. The building went through several uses over the centuries but is now partly a handicrafts centre and partly a restaurant serving traditional home cooked Turkish meals. These meals are different to what you get in Turkish restaurants with the emphasis on a much more authentic experience rather than the meaty affair that most of us are used to.

Inside the rooms, you will find drawings of what life inside the madrasa must have been like when it was still used to teach young Ottoman students. The main courtyard also has a bust of Sinan in it – although this representation of human form is still jarring when you bear in mind the orthodox nature of the building itself.

Tourist sites can often give a warped view of a culture or people and so having a location like this to showcase traditional Turkish handicrafts, arts and even food is a great way of giving visitors a different experience than what they would normally be used to.

Looking around this modest building, one cannot be helped but be impressed by the fact that even unknown functionaries like Cafer Aga were keen to do good works to secure their afterlife and to aim for excellence when doing so.

Sokullu Mehmet Pasha Mosque:

Never Bring Work Home

Mehmed Pasha Sokolovic was of Serbian origin and served as Grand vizier to three Ottoman sultans, starting with Suleiman the Magnificent. From a poor Christian boy to one of the most powerful Muslim rulers in the world, Mehmed Pasha lived a rollercoaster life. Mehmed Pasha was an extremely able and talented vizier, even managing to hide the death of Sultan Suleiman for several months until Selim II was able to reach him from Kütahya. He also virtually ran the Empire while Selim II and his successor Murad III spent more time in the harem.

Apart from his political skill, he was also a great builder. He ordered the construction of an eponymous bridge in his home region in Serbia. He also built the Vizier's Bridge in Podgorica, the capital of Montenegro, the Black Mosque (later converted into a Church) in Sofia, Bulgaria and the Azapkapi Mosque in Istanbul. He also took a special interest in spreading Islam and Ottoman influence in the Far East, sending expeditions to the island of Sumatra in present day Indonesia.

But Mehmed Pasha became a victim of his own efficiency. A deranged dervish turned up at his door one day. Even though it was the private office of the Grand Vizier rather than his official office and it was not during office hours, he went out to meet him. Almost anyone else, even a dozen ranks below would have refused to do so. But Mehmed Pasha was a workaholic and thought the most efficient thing to do was to deal with him there and then. The dervish found the Grand Vizier without his usual bodyguard and assassinated him.

Sokullu Mehmed Pasha was a hardworking and loyal Grand Vizier who could have set the Empire on the course of more success and victory, but due to the blade of an unknown assassin joined the ranks of the martyrs instead. In the 16 years following his assassination, the Sultan would change Grand Viziers no less than 10 times due to desperately searching for someone who could live up to his high standards. Little wonder that more and more future leaders would keep a healthy distance between themselves and the public.

Fragments of the Black Stone:

True or false?

According to Islamic history, the Black Stone (Hajr Al-Aswad) is one of two heavenly jewels that fell to Earth. The other is the Maqam ("station") of Ibrahim (AS.) Situated in the holy Kaaba in the Grand Mosque of Makkah, the Black Stone is the focal point of the Muslim world with every circumambulation around the Kaaba starting and ending with it.

Yet almost a thousand years ago, a sect called the Qaramita erupted out of Bahrain and attacked the Hajj pilgrims. At the end of their massacre, they had not satiated their unholy thirst for vengeance, and they decided to tear the Black Stone out of the Kaaba and take it back to Bahrain. It remained there for a few years after which it was returned due to pressure from the Abbasid and Fatimid caliphs – possibly the only example of these two rival families working together.

When it was returned dramatically during Friday prayers at the Kufa grand mosque, it was broken into several pieces. While the majority were inset into an ambergris paste and set in a silver case (as we see it today) some pieces of the stone remain missing.

These missing pieces have given rise to legends over the years that stray pieces of stones are part of the Black Stone. None of these legends have been proven and almost all are certainly false as there is no provenance or evidence to suggest their veracity.

Examples of these legends in Istanbul can be found in the mihrab of the Sultanahmet Mosque, on the keystone of the tomb of Sultan Suleiman the Magnificent and in the Sokullu Mehmet Pasha Mosque. They are almost certainly false legends as few, if any, contemporary records survive detailing these stones as being from the Kaaba or even how they managed to find their way to Istanbul.

Museum of the History of Science and Technology in Islam:

Dreamers and Doers

For more than a few centuries, Muslims have been fed a steady diet of propaganda depicting Western superiority and their own inferiority in all technological and scientific matters. We were taught to believe that we contributed little to the world. Our golden age was relabelled the Dark Ages. Naturally, this had the desired impact, leaving a Muslim world demoralised.

However, a late intellectual awakening is taking place with Muslims "rediscovering" their own vital place in shaping the modern world. Articles, books and documentaries have been produced highlighting the advances that Muslims pioneered long before the Reconquista, the Reformation and the Renaissance.

This Museum located in Gülhane Park is one such attempt at correcting the imbalance in knowledge of our own heritage. It is largely the brainchild of Professor Fuat Sezgin, an Orientalist at the Goethe University in Frankfurt. On a visit to Istanbul, the Professor saw the newly refurbished Ottoman stables in Gülhane Park and realised that they would be the perfect setting for an exhibition he was working on. He contacted the municipal government and eventually convinced the governor and then the Prime Minister to support his project.

The museum itself displays relatively few artefacts compared to equivalent scientific museums in other world capitals. Many of these items are imagined or approximations from scant descriptions. This is instructive; as while the items themselves are impressive, their paucity is an indicator of the relative lack of importance that the Ottomans and their contemporaries in the Muslim world gave to scientific and technological advancement.

Ayasofya:

The Imperial Mosque par excellence

Ayasofya was the Imperial Mosque of choice for much of the history of the Ottoman Empire. Not only was it the grandest Mosque in Istanbul, it was also ideally located right next to Topkapi Palace. It would be the location for the Sultan to attend his Friday prayers in procession, but even other daily prayers would be attended via the side entrance that allowed him access to his private loge.

Three times a week, the ministers of state, including the Grand Vizier, would come to the Ayasofya for Fajr prayers before dawn. After they finished praying in congregation, they would proceed on to the Palace and the audience chamber for their cabinet meetings with the Sultan to discuss affairs of state.

Ayasofya: Church, Mosque, Museum...

Will the real Ayasofya Please Stand Up?

Ayasofya is arguably one of the most beautiful buildings in the world and inarguably one of the most contested. The story of this place of worship spans multiple empires, faiths and purposes. Originally built as the Church of the Holy Wisdom centuries before the birth of the Prophet ﷺ, it was destroyed twice during riots in the Byzantine Empire. The third version of the church and the building that we see today was built by the Emperor Justinian.

For almost a thousand years, this was the seat of Eastern Christendom and arguably the greatest Church in the world; the venue for crowning Emperors and sanctifying Orthodox Popes. The soaring dome, the gigantic mosaics and the sheer size of the building spoke to the magnificence of the Empire that built it. It is no wonder that when Emperor Justinian entered the newly finished building, he exclaimed, "Solomon, I have outdone thee!"

When Constantinople was conquered by Sultan Mehmet Fatih, the Byzantine Empire did not survive but the Ayasofya did. The Sultan himself visited the building and gave thanks to Allah for his victory. The Church, like the rest of the public buildings in the city, were taken over according to the military norms of the day and in accordance with Islamic rules of conquest for cities that did not surrender. There is evidence to suggest that the Sultan made doubly sure of the legality of the takeover by paying for the building with his own private funds.

Within days, it was converted to an Imperial Mosque. Mehmet made the building a Waqf (Islamic endowment) and, in foreshadowing words, laid a curse on anyone who attempted to change it from being a mosque by saying that none but a tyrant would attempt to do so.

When Istanbul was occupied by the allied forces after the end of the first World War, it was feared that the European armies would convert the Ayasofya back into a church. Sultan Mehmed VI gave instructions to his bodyguards to ring the building with dynamite and should anyone attempt to convert it into a church, they should destroy it. Better it no longer exists than it no longer be a mosque.

Enter Mustafa Kemal. In his drive to extinguish many Islamic practices from the deceased Ottoman Empire and to gain favour from his former colonial adversaries, he changed the mosque into a museum. It was a deeply polarising move but one in keeping with the nationalistic fervour sweeping through the Muslim world.

More than 80 years later, parts of the Muslim world are realising that they do not need to choose between imperialism and dictatorship, between the past and the future or between their faith and their place in the civilised world. The Ayasofya could be a mosque and a museum. As Winston Churchill pointed out, "we shape our buildings, thereafter they shape us.

Ayasofya Grounds:

Thomas Whittemore Had a Dream

Whilst walking around the grounds of the Ayasofya, you will see some of the excavated remnants of previous incarnations of the Byzantine church. While it is clear how the Church became a Mosque after the conquest of Constantinople by Sultan Mehmet Fatih, it is not clear at all how the Mosque became a museum.

Some Western academics and statesmen dreamed of returning Istanbul to its Byzantine glory. They saw Muslim rule as the Reconquista had seen the Moorish rule of Andalusia: an aberration that could be reversed and eventually erased.

Thomas Whittemore was one such American scholar. He had a huge influence on the way Ayasofya looks today. Unlike most historians and archaeologists, he intended to influence the course of events and not merely document them.

Thomas Whittemore was enamoured with all things Byzantine and was fascinated by their modern-day heirs – the Russians. He spent many years indulging his pro-Russian tendencies and did considerable work for the Russian Relief commission. However, it was a friendship with Mustafa Kemal that would help make his dream into reality.

After a brief and surprisingly easy lobbying period, he was able to convince his friend to hand over to his team one of the greatest mosques in the world to bring out the mosaics, remove the carpets and trappings of the mosque. Even he was surprised by how successful he was: "Santa Sophia was a mosque the day that I talked to him. The next morning, when I went to the mosque, there was a sign on the door written in Ataturk's own hand. It said: 'The *museum* is closed for repairs.'"

Thomas Whittemore is the embodiment of a man who dreamt with his eyes wide open; not just sitting back and wishing things were different. He planned, he worked and did not stop until his goal was achieved. People like him changed one of the most iconic mosques in the world, into a museum and it would take people like that to change it back.

Ayasofya:

Evolution not revolution

The fall of the Ottoman Empire sent shockwaves throughout the Muslim world. One of the most potent symbols of that fall was the conversion of the Grand Mosque of Istanbul, the Ayasofya, into a museum. To faithful Muslims from across the world, visiting the Ayasofya left many with a feeling of humiliation especially because they were not allowed to pray there.

It was impossible to avoid comparison with the Grand Mosque of Cordoba, which also does not allow Muslim prayer and now houses over 50 chapels after the Reconquista. The Ayasofya used to be a symbol of the Ottoman Empire, triumphant and confident over the Byzantine Empire. Now it was a symbol of the victory of Nationalism and Kemalism in post-Ottoman Türkiye.

The survival and the eventual revival of Islam in the Republic is a fascinating story involving immense sacrifice at all levels, from a martyred Prime Minister to the humble Anatolian peasantry. However, the revival did not take the form of a messy or bloody revolution as it did in most other post-colonial Muslim states. Instead, it was marked by its slow, ponderous almost evolutionary pace.

Islam was preserved in the rural heartlands and as those heartlands grew in number and economic power, so did their political reach. Whenever the institutions of Kemalism, often the military, pushed back through coups or repression, instead of forcing an existential battle or civil war, the Islamic current would take one step back, regroup and simply try again. Eventually, they could not be pushed back anymore.

This approach can be seen with the Ayasofya. There had always been calls for it to be converted back to a Mosque, but the process was surprisingly slow and deliberate. First, they discreetly opened a small antechamber to become a mini-Mosque near the Sultans entrance. Then they broadcast the Adhaan from the minarets. Eventually, they held Quran recitals in the building during Ramadan.

They understood what many of their compatriots elsewhere do not – evolution is better than revolution. Evolution is a slow and natural process where decisions are made in pace with societal norms rather than messy revolutions that may not have the backing of the public. When President Erdogan converted the building back into a place of worship, there was much rejoicing and some consternation. The Ayasofya continues to be a potent symbol of the state of the nation it is in.

Mosaics in Ayasofya:

Islamic Tolerance

Converting the Ayasofya into a working mosque meant that the Byzantine mosaics needed to be removed. Islam has strict rules on images of living creatures that even the most iconoclastic Byzantine Emperor would have struggled to contend with. Instead of destroying these beautiful mosaics, the Muslims decided to cover them up. This way, the mosaics were not visible, but they still existed. There was no other reason to go through the trouble to do this apart from tolerance of other faiths.

In the 1800s, Sultan Abdul Mejid I even ordered the entire Ayasofya to be refurbished including the Byzantine mosaics that had been hidden under the plaster. After the refurbishment, the mosaics were covered once more, and the building continued to be used as a mosque.

It is worth reflecting on this when looking at the various mosaics. Tolerance and respect of others was the hallmark of Islamic civilization and people; it did not come to destroy the history and achievements of other people, instead it came to build upon them and take it to newer heights. There have been exceptions, but they have been just that – exceptions. The mosaics of Ayasofya are just one example of the tolerance that exemplified our past.

The Dome of Ayasofya:

Confidence and the Rebuilding of the Dome

In architectural circles, domes are sometimes referred to as "the kings of all roofs." This is not just because of their majestic beauty appreciated by all, but also because building a beautiful dome is a bit of an architectural nightmare that needs complex engineering to help distribute the weight evenly and prevent collapse. The dome of Ayasofya should be seen as one of the wonders of the ancient world. The largest dome to be built for more than a thousand years (apart from a few hiccups) it has withstood the test of time and has had a profound influence on the design of domes in the Islamic world.

During the late Byzantine period, the dome of Ayasofya became unstable. Unfortunately, the Byzantine Empire had fallen on difficult times and no one in the Empire had the knowledge or skills to fix it. The Byzantine Emperor was forced to approach his archenemy, Sultan Murad II, and ask for help.

Even though they were technically enemies, Sultan Murad II showed his chivalrous side and in an acknowledgement to the special place that Ayasofya occupied in world architecture, he sent his best engineer to fix the dome. He secured the structure and made necessary refurbishments to the building.

When the engineer returned to Sultan Murad II and was asked how things had gone, the engineer replied, "I have repaired and refurbished their dome ... and have also laid the foundations for our minarets." The court erupted in laughter, and the Sultan smiled. The Ottomans were certainly not lacking in confidence. It showed before they won the physical battle, they had won the psychological one.

The minarets of Ayasofya:

Saving the minarets

The minarets of Ayasofya were scheduled to be destroyed by the revolutionary government of Mustafa Kemal. This was in keeping with its new designation as a museum, in which case the minarets would be redundant. The minarets were also an unwelcome reminder of the previous conquest of Constantinople by the Muslim armies; they had to go. The destruction of minarets had already taken place at a few of the other mosques that were converted to museums.

The order to carry out the necessary preparations for a clean and orderly demolition of the minarets was sent to an engineering professor. Being a pious man with an understanding of the religious and historical value of the minarets, he became incredibly depressed at the thought of having to carry out this order that did not sit well with his intellect or his soul. He could not refuse the order outright as it would bring severe consequences for him and his family.

While sitting in a coffee house pondering what to do, another lecturer at the same university asked him why he looked so forlorn. When he explained the situation, his friend smiled and replied, "Don't worry; simply send back a report saying that should any of the minarets be touched, the whole dome would collapse as they are structurally reinforcing each other."

The professor did so, and the government immediately dropped the idea fearing the structural integrity of the Ayasofya was at risk. Although silenced for decades, the minarets still stand today and now, once again, call to prayer. A faithful heart combined with a quick brain is a potent combination to not only glorify the Creator but, in this case, be a great benefit in the service of the Creation.

The Roundels of Ayasofya:

They Cost a Prime Minister his Life

The roundels, like almost every Ottoman Mosque, displays the names of the Prophet ﷺ, the first four Caliphs and the two grandsons of the Prophet (SAW.) They were made by the master calligrapher Kazasker Mustafa İzzet Efendi. Interestingly, his other notable work hangs in the Washington monument in Washington D.C. – a gift fom an Old Empire to a new one.

When the mosque was converted into a museum at the time of Mustafa Kemal, the roundels were taken off and scheduled for destruction. Due to some reason, more than likely a faithful employee hoping to save them, the order was never carried out and they were hidden in storage for many years.

When Adnan Menderes came to power in the 1950's, he made concessions to Islam in the public space. He allowed the call to prayer to be made in Arabic and he eased off on the crackdown on Imam Hatip schools. For these reasons as well as his disdain for the hyper-secular elite of Turkish society, he had drawn the ire of the Turkish army who saw themselves as the guardians of Kemalism.

In addition to all this, Menderes ordered that the calligraphic roundels of Ayasofya be placed back in their original place. Partly due to this and other concessions he made to Islam in Turkish society; the army carried out a coup against him. It would be the first of many. In 1961, the military coup leaders hanged him and two of his ministers – Fatin Zorlu and Hasan Polatkan.

When you look up at these beautiful works of art – and faith – hung up all around Ayasofya, remember that they survived only because there were people brave enough to stand up to tyranny – and that even a Prime Minister paid with his life for them to remain in their rightful place.

The Library of Mahmud I:

The Mosque of Holy Wisdom

Mahmud I ascended to the throne when his extravagant uncle Ahmed III was deposed. Eager to break with the past and avoid any appearance of excess, Mahmud I spent his wealth in areas that would be unlikely to anger the common man. He ordered extensive renovations of the Ayasofya including the addition of an imaret (soup kitchen), school and the library.

Previously libraries had often been the preserve of rich patrons and out of the reach of common people. Mahmud I reversed this process and donated his precious books to the public library at Ayasofya. Seeing the Sultan do so, many other wealthy Ottomans did so as well. "Aya Sofia" literally means "Holy Wisdom" in the Greek language. Fittingly, with the addition of a library, the Church of Holy Wisdom had now become the Mosque of Holy Wisdom.

Although the books have since been relocated to the Süleymaniye Mosque and the library is now empty, there is still something that can be gained from visiting this library. The doors of the library contain the inscription, "Ya Fattah" – literally, "O Opener!" It is one of the 99 names of Allah and a particular favourite for entrances in Ottoman buildings. It is also a fitting inscription for anyone who seeks to gain wisdom.

Information is easily available to anyone with an internet connection these days, but knowledge is only for those who can process that information into something meaningful. Wisdom, on the other hand, is for the lucky few who open their mind to how they can use knowledge to change things.

Enrico Dandolo Tomb Marker:

The Crusade Against Christians

Enrico Dandolo was the ruler of Venice. He was totally blind, but this did not stop him from playing an active role on the world stage. As the head of one of the wealthiest and most powerful city states, he was chosen as the leader of the Fourth Crusade. The mightiest armies of Europe had been vanquished by Salahuddin at the horns of Hattin and lost the prize of Jerusalem at the end of the Third Crusade. It was time for a rematch.

The blind Dandolo and his army were less-than-holy warriors. They travelled to Palestine via Byzantium and seeing all the wealth of their Orthodox Christian friends, decided Jerusalem could wait. Instead, they attacked Constantinople itself and because their defences were down – not expecting to be attacked by fellow Christians – it was a bloodbath.

Legend has it that when Dandolo died, he was buried in a crypt in Ayasofya near where you see the marker of his name. After the Crusaders had left and the Byzantines had regained control, they would often spit at the tomb. However, it was discovered later on that there was no body entombed there. The marker was inexplicably left in place, however.

Above all else, Dandolo is evidence of the brutality of the Crusades. Being a former ambassador to Constantinople and knowing of the enormous wealth in the city, he led the Crusade to sack this bastion of Eastern Christianity, put the civilians to the sword and even mockingly crowned a prostitute as the Eastern Orthodox Pope. The great riches of Constantinople, from the relics to the ornamentation of churches, were ripped out and transported to Venice where you can see many of them in churches like St Marks.

When Sultan Mehmet Fatih laid siege to the city centuries later, Eastern Orthodox priests openly stated, "better the turban of the Turk than the mitre of Rome." There could hardly be a greater testament to the tolerance and humanity that exemplified previous Islamic civilizations.

Omphalion:

The Last Byzantine – Constantine XI Palaeologus

In the carpeted hall of the Ayasofya mosque, there is an area that allows the marble to be exposed. This is the Omphalion. The Omphalion was the exact spot where the Byzantine Emperor was crowned. The Byzantine Emperor or Empress were some of the most powerful people in the world for more than a millennium.

Although the empire started off being ruled by towering personalities like Constantine and Justinian, the Byzantine Empire had eventually degenerated into repeated abdications, coups and regicides. In fact, it became so difficult to keep track of the power dynamics that the term *Byzantine* is now used to describe any process following a particularly devious and difficult path.

The last Byzantine Emperor was Constantine XI Palaeologus. Although personally brave, he could not hold back the Muslims any longer. During the conquest of Constantinople, he died fighting alongside his men such that it was difficult to tell with any certainty which of the fallen was the Emperor.

His heroic end inspired his people. Stories were told about how he evaded death and was biding his time for the right moment to strike back at the "infidel" Turks. He is even sometimes referred to as "the marble Emperor" as legend states that he was turned into marble and will be reanimated when his people need him most.

While the Byzantine public were putting their hope in myths, the possible heirs to the Byzantine throne were on a completely different course. Constantine had two nephews, but rather than be crowned at the Omphalion like their ancestors, they reverted to Islam and became pashas in the court of Fatih.

Hope for an awaited saviour who will rescue his people from the abyss will be quite familiar to Muslims too. In the present day, when disaster follows disaster and there seems no way out – many have resorted to the same paralytic fatalism and rather than take proactive steps to change, simply await the arrival of the Mahdi. The truth is clear, winners do not wait for others to save them.

Selim II Tombs:

Winning the Ottoman Game of Thrones

These beautiful tombs in the grounds of the Ayasofya complex belong to a succession of Ottoman Sultans. The first is that of Selim II. Selim II was the winner of the Ottoman 'Game of Thrones'. It was one of the grimmest contests in their entire history: the race to see who would inherit the Empire of Suleiman the Magnificent. Suffering tragic betrayals, severe disease and summary executions, heir after heir had perished, leaving the road clear for Selim to ascend to the throne on Suleiman's death.

He is often portrayed as frivolous and degenerate, but the reality is that he was being judged not against his contemporaries but in comparison to the ten giants that preceded him.

It is true, however, that Selim II was the first Sultan not to lead his troops into battle, preferring to leave the messy work of conquest to others. In this he marked the start of the sedentary Sultans who were more interested in pleasure than the business of governing.

Selim's reign saw a string of defeats for the Empire – an unusual experience for the usually victorious Ottomans – yet they were able to shrug it off as their position remained overwhelmingly dominant. They thought this was all just a blip. Little did they know it presaged what was to come.

To understand how much had changed, we need only look at his nickname: while his father was known as "the Magnificent", Selim was nicknamed "the Blonde" or – less charitably – "the drunk." He died after a slip in the bathroom caused him to sustain a severe head injury and likely brain haemorrhage. Some say the Sultan slipped on the polished wet marble floor, while others say that he was so drunk he could not stand straight. Whatever the true reason was, it did not bode well for the Empire.

Selim II Tombs:

No Honour amongst Thieves

If you look closely at the tilework that adorns the building of the Selim II tomb, you will see that they are slightly faded. This is because they are not originals but replicas.

During the 1890's, the dentist of Sultan Abdul Hamid II, convinced the Ottoman Government that experts in France would be able to restore the tilework and renovate them. The trusting Ottomans took out an entire section of priceless Iznik tiles and gave it to him and they were temporarily replaced by these low-quality replicas made in Sèvres, France.

However, in an act of typical colonial era theft, Albert Dorigny never returned with the tiles and instead gave them to the Louvre Museum in Paris where they are displayed to this day. Often, certain nations present themselves as morally superior to the rest of the world by their upholding of values such as liberty, equality and fraternity; but a stroll through any of their museums will reveal a treasure trove of stolen artefacts and thievery that would put even the most low-life gangsters to shame.

Despite repeated calls by the Turkish government for the return of these priceless tiles stolen under false pretences, there is no sign that the French government is about return them. The fake tiles at the tomb of Selim II stand mute testimony as to who has real moral superioriy.

Introduction to Topkapi

Standing at the gates of Topkapı, what you are about to enter is the most well-preserved ancient Muslim palace you will ever see and quite possibly the most important one still standing. Topkapı palace is a museum today but was a living and breathing seat of Government in the not-too-distant past. The fate of hundreds of millions from Baghdad to the Balkans was decided within its walls. The ripples of history spread out from this location throughout the Muslim world–for good or for worse. The empty halls and the bare walls can only give us the briefest glimpse into the consequential nature of the work that went on here.

Unlike the concept of palaces that most of us have grown up with, a Muslim palace was rarely a single building, but an organic structure with pavilions and buildings added in different eras and to commemorate different events. The palace was not just the home of the emperor; it was the location of the most exclusive University, the seat of Government and the repository of the nation's wealth and historical artefacts. Imagine the White House, the Senate, Harvard University, Fort Knox and the Smithsonian all rolled into one location, and you begin to get an idea of what Topkapı meant in its heyday.

The original name of the palace, used to differentiate it from the previous palace that Mehmet Fatih had built, was the wonderfully uninventive "The New Palace."

The problem with such a name is that a few hundred years in and the "New Palace" is not quite so new anymore. Then an even bigger problem arose. The Sultan had a newer palace than the New Palace built on the banks of Bosphorus. A solution had to be found.

The solution was to rename the palace as "Topkapı" (Turkish for Cannon Gate) after one of its most imposing gates of the palace. To add more confusion to the name, the Topkapı gate itself no longer exists. The name has still stuck ever since, even if it is a relatively modern construction.

Sultan Ahmed III Fountain:

Sultan Ahmed III

Every dynasty has a ruler during whose rule the height of luxury and arts is attained. For the Bourbon French, it was Louis XIV or 'the Sun King'. For the British, it was the Georgian era. For the Ottomans, it was the reign of Ahmed III. This period was known as the "Tulip Era" with this flower becoming ever-present and selling for vast amounts of money, much like fine art today. It became so emblematic that even to this day, the image of the tulip bud is almost shorthand for the Turkish nation.

The Tulip era (Lâle Devri) abounded in increasingly far-fetched acts of devotion to arts and culture. In fact, in the garden of the Grand Vizier, the place of each 4th tulip was sometimes taken by a candle of the same colour and height so that the flowers could be enjoyed even in the darkness of the night.

However, it was not all play. It was Sultan Ahmed III and his Grand Vizier who came the closest to totally defeating the mortal enemy of the Ottomans: Russia. A victory that would have altered the course of history was prevented when the treacherous Safavids of Persia made preparations to stab the Ottomans in the back and invade them from the West. The army was recalled and the Russians lived to fight another day.

Although he was a patron of the arts and sciences – Ahmed III was eventually overthrown due to a variety of factors including his spendthrift ways. The peaceful transfer of power has been a trait that has eluded Muslims from almost the very beginning of our history. So, when it came time for Ahmed III to be deposed, everyone expected bloodshed and a fight. Instead, Ahmed III graciously pledged allegiance to his nephew and retired to house imprisonment in Topkapı palace. Thus, the beautiful Tulip era ended as beautifully as it started.

Sultan Ahmed III Fountain:

The Concerns of a Sultan

In a faith that makes charity a pillar of worship, there is one act of charity that is given pride of place. The Prophet ﷺ had emphasised that providing water is the best of charitable acts. Reflecting on this, it becomes obvious why this is the case. While a human being can survive for months without shelter and days without food, a lack of water will lead to a swift demise.

Ever since then, any person of prominence who could not build a mosque, would opt to have a fountain installed instead. Fountains can be found everywhere you go in Istanbul, from the labyrinthine streets of the Grand Bazaar to intersections in residential areas.

As the palace was like a small city within a city and many hundreds of people went to the palace for petitions or requests, Sultan Ahmed III had a large and beautiful fountain installed just outside Topkapı palace. Not only did it provide drinking water for all those coming to and fro during hot days, but during Eid festivals, it would dispense sherbet.

The inscriptions running across like a band near the top are a poem, part of which is composed by Sultan Ahmed III himself, and asks all who drink from the fountain to pray for his soul. It is interesting to note that even the Sultan was cognisant of his eventual passage to the next life where his riches and power would be of no use.

Bab-i-Humayun (The Imperial Gate):

The Most Famous Door in the World

This is the first gate that you will come across and it was built by Mehmet Fatih. The gate used to have a Royal Lodge or viewing room on top of it from where the Sultan and the female members of his household would be able to watch processions and ceremonies without being disturbed. Unfortunately, this was eventually destroyed and never replaced.

The Tughra at the centre of the gate is that of Sultan Abdul Aziz who had the gate refurbished during his reign. It is worth taking a second to view the calligraphic panels overhead. The angled calligraphy is a unique masterpiece inscribed with verses from the Quran.

The panel immediately below it also has part of a Quranic verse that the early Ottomans took to heart as they swept all before them: "Victory is from Allah, Conquest is near, so give glad tidings to the believers O Muhammad."

Governments are often referred to by the name of the building they are located in or by the entrance door of such a building. For example, the government of the United States of America is often referred to as the White House and the British Government as No. 10 Downing Street.

The Ottoman Government was known throughout Europe and most of the World as "the Sublime Porte" – a rough French Translation of Bab-i-Ali (The High Gate) that was the threshold of Topkapı Palace. It became shorthand for the Ottoman state and government. All major announcements and firmans from the Sultan would be read at this door since Topkapı Palace was the seat of Government as well as the private residence of the Sultan.

In later centuries, the Sultan became less and less interested in governing and more in enjoying the trappings of luxury within the palace. The Grand Vizier and other ministers were asked to move down the road to another building. The entrance to that building became known as the new Sublime Porte. Meanwhile, the old Bab-i-Ali that you see, was renamed as Bab-i-Humayun – "the Imperial Gate."

Power and authority reside not in a title, but in the person who makes the decisions. Many a Sultan had enough titles to fill multiple pages, but they were not the masters of their destiny. They were controlled by Viziers, ministers and even concubines who could bend them to their will by manipulation or misinformation. The Imperial gate serves as a reminder that making difficult decisions in difficult circumstances is the price of power. If you give up one, you will eventually lose the other.

Gate of Salutation:

The Biggest Fool in the World

If you look to the right of the Gate of Salutation (Bab-i-salaam), you will see a fountain and some odd sized marble columns. This is where the head gardener would wash his tools. The head gardener also doubled up as the executioner –quite the varied job description! The marble stumps were used to display the heads of his unfortunate victims.

There is a story that a wandering and particularly filthy looking poor dervish was once questioned by the new Grand Vizier. Looking for a chance to have some laughs at the expense of the Dervish, he asked him "Who is the biggest fool in the World?" Without skipping a beat, the Dervish replied, "You are, of course." The enraged Grand Vizier demanded to know why he gave such an impertinent reply. "Because, O Grand Vizier, you have coveted this role for years and now have attained it even though you had to go past the decapitated head of your predecessor and that of his predecessor to get it."

The Grand Vizier dismissed him, but it was too late. Sometime later, his own head joined that of the previous Viziers on the columns outside Bab-i-Salaam, the traditional display area for heads of those who had fallen spectacularly from favour.

The Dervish knew that we often desire something that could be bad for us. Truly, it is a mercy from Allah that we do not have every prayer fulfilled for we do not know what is truly good for us and where every wish will lead to. In the deathly serious world of global politics during the Ottoman era, the rewards were massive – but so were the risks. Play the game right and you could write your name on the pages of history in golden letters. Make a mistake and you may find your head resting outside the Gate of Salutation.

Hagia Irene Church:

A Church in the Heart of the Islamic world

This building has so many incarnations that it could rival Dr Who. It started life as a pagan temple, then became the first church of the Byzantine Empire, it was eventually repurposed as a military warehouse, transformed into a museum before finally becoming a concert hall.

The Emperor Constantine is rumoured to have founded three main churches in Constantinople: Hagia Sophia (Ayasofya), the Church of Holy Wisdom; Hagia Dynamis, the Church of Holy Power; and Hagia Irene, the Church of Holy Peace.

Of these three – the only surviving one is Hagia Irene. Even after the conquest of Constantinople, the Muslims never converted this church to a mosque. This was even more surprising given its location in the Sultan's own front lawn. It would be like walking into the Vatican to find an untouched mosque in the corner of St Peter's Square.

Ottoman tolerance was not just about the survival of a few churches in Istanbul. It was woven into the very fabric of their society. In the later years of the Empire, the evils of nationalism and sectarianism tore apart this fabric. In a world that is increasingly polarised, Hagia Irene – the Church of the Holy Peace – stands in the seat of Caliphate as a silent witness to a more harmonious and peaceful time.

The Imperial Kitchens:

The Origin of the Meze

While there are many perks to being Sultan, there are also risks and constrictions that come with it too. The constant threat of assassination, the protocols and the formalities are the price one must pay for the crown.

Poisoning was always a threat to an Emperor, therefore when Sultan Suleiman the Magnificent defeated the Persians, he took home with him their food tasters. They were a common sight in Persian courts since poisoning was not unusual amongst them.

But Suleiman did not like the idea of someone eating from the same plate as he did, so he asked that samples from each dish be given to the food tasters. They could do their job and the Sultan did not have to eat their leftovers. This selection of dishes became known as the Meze and eventually high society copied the Sultan even though they had no food tasters – or anyone trying to poison them for that matter. So, if this story is to be believed, the origin of the Meze dishes lies in the paranoia of Sultan Suleiman the Magnificent. A tasty outcome as I am sure all will agree.

The Imperial Kitchens:

The Honesty of Sinners

In a famous hadith of the Prophet ﷺ, it was narrated that Muslims should not eat or drink from vessels of gold or silver. "Whoever eats and drinks from vessels of gold and silver, is taking fire from Hell into his belly" (Sahih Muslim). Notwithstanding the severity of this prohibition, some Ottoman Sultans were unable to abide by this rule, despite their lofty titles as Caliph, Sultan and Shadow of God on Earth.

Yet even Sultans did not want to flout Islamic law in Ramadan. To make up for not being able to use golden vessels, they had yellow Chinese porcelain dishes made. If they could not have gold, at least a golden colour would do. There is an interesting lesson here: the Sultans could easily have had a fatwa declared stating that it was permissible for them to eat on gold using some flimsy pretext or other. More brazenly, they could have just flouted the law in Ramadan just like they did outside it.

Instead, what this yellow porcelain dish signifies is that the Sultans admitted they were sinning by eating on gold and that they would at least try and make amends during Ramadan. By admitting that aspects of their lifestyle contravene the letter and spirit of Islam, they did not attempt to bend the faith to justify their actions. With this honesty, there is hope for reformation. Without it, there is none.

Imperial Council Chamber:
The Golden Grille

Standing in the Imperial Council chamber, you are now in the heart of the Ottoman government – akin to the cabinet room of the British government or the Situation Room of the White House. Three days a week, the Ottoman Council would meet in this room after Fajr prayer. The Grand Vizier and the other ministers would meet at the Ayasofya for Fajr and after this would ride down to Topkapı Palace.

There they would meet with the Sultan and decide on affairs of state. One day a commoner barged into the council room. Looking around the room, he said "Which of you fortunate souls is the Sultan?"

The Sultan felt humiliated and decided that from then on, he would no longer physically attend council meetings as this was beneath the dignity of his title. Instead, he would view the meeting from a grilled high window. You can see the window opening directly above where the Council would sit.

Sultans soon discovered another advantage of their new seating arrangement. Since no one could see if the Sultan was there or not, they had to assume he was. This meant the Sultan could start skipping Imperial Council Meetings should he choose to and yet be sure that none of his ministers would step out of line.

Unfortunately, what started as an attempt to preserve the dignity of the Sultan ended up becoming an excuse for Sultans to just stop attending Council meetings. Soon, they gave up even pretending to attend meetings and left many of the affairs of state to others, only interjecting when they could be bothered. Without strong leadership, the empire began to shake and then crumble.

Imperial Council Chamber:

Who is Behind the Curtain?

The date is 2nd of September 1651, the 16th of Ramadan 1061 AH. The location is the Imperial Council chamber. It is an extraordinary scene. The room is filled with the highest viziers of the Ottoman Empire. It is a hive of activity with the Kapudan Pasha who controlled the Ottoman navy, the Shaikh-ul-Islam who was the highest religious authority, the Kizlar Agha who ran the treasury, the commanders of the army and the Jannisaries, all present.

Presiding over them all is Siyavus Pasha, the Grand Vizier. They have come together for this extraordinary session in order to discuss a terrible accusation against Kosem Sultan. She is being accused of trying to depose or even kill the Sultan (her own grandson). She is present too, but in keeping with harem rules, is behind a thick curtain.

The meeting is the highpoint of a bitter power struggle between Kosem and Turhan – her daughter in law and the mother of the current Sultan. For many months and years now, they have been building up rival power bases before making the final move on their rival. Now the time had come.

The meeting swayed one way then the other as viziers made impassioned pleas and special witnesses were called forth. Eventually, it became clear that Turhan had managed to produce a couple of aces and convince the viziers that it was time to get rid of Kosem. As the meeting became more and more heated, accusations and even insults were hurled at the Buyuk Valide Sultan, to give Kosem her official title.

This was unthinkable only days ago. Kosem had ruled the Ottoman Empire for decades as the wife, mother and grandmother of Sultans. She had established it on a firm footing on the international stage, she had opened charitable projects throughout the Empire and every powerful man in the Empire owed their career to her. In fact, even her arch-rival Turhan Sultan herself was brought into the palace by Kosem.

Initially, the assembled leaders thought she was stunned into silence at hearing anyone raise their voice to her. Then, they became suspicious and when one of them gathered enough courage and checked behind the curtain, they realised that Kosem had run away halfway through the meeting. They sent the guards after her and eventually found her hiding inside a chest of scarves in her private room. She was caught and strangled with her own hair. Kosem Sultan, the grandmother of the current Sultan and the real power behind the throne for the reign of four sultans was no more. And at that exact moment, Turhan was being named the regent for her son in that same Imperial council chamber where some dreams were made, and others were shattered.

Imperial Council Chamber:
The Final Meeting

It is worth considering that this room has seen some momentous decisions take place that impacted the lives of millions of people – sometimes even to this day. Deposing a Sultan, declaring war and agreeing armistices – all these decisions would have been taken in this very room. If the walls could talk, what would they say?

The final council meeting to take place in the Imperial Council Chamber took place a significant period after Topkapı Palace had been abandoned. Murad V had come to the throne after his uncle Sultan Abdul Aziz was dethroned in suspicious circumstances. Within days, the ex-Sultan Abdul Aziz was killed, no doubt to ensure that he no longer posed a threat to the new Sultan Murad V, or more importantly to those who had deposed him.

Murad V was a pawn in the hands of those who had orchestrated the coup against Sultan Abdul Aziz. What they had not realised was that their pawn was mentally deranged and an alcoholic. Murad V suffered public panic attacks and struggled with even the most basic of meetings.

The Imperial council was considering deposing Murad V in August of 1876 and needed a venue that was far from the new palace and interfering ears. The old council chamber was the perfect location as no one would look for them there.

The council deliberated and finally agreed that Murad V could no longer continue on the throne. They therefore decided on his more reasonable (and sober) half-brother Abdul Hamid II. They felt certain that he would be just as easy to manipulate as his half-brother. Judging by the fact that this was the last meeting this room has seen, they could not have been more wrong.

Imperial Armoury:

From Swords to Apple peelers

One of the most important roles of any government is to look after the safety and security of their citizens. The original use of the Imperial Armoury was to serve as the national bank of the Ottoman Empire where officials and Janissaries would be paid. It is now used to display the extensive collection of military artefacts from the Ottoman Empire, but even has items going as far back as the Umayyads and spanning many of the empires in between.

There is a display showing the evolution of the Sultan's sword. On one end are the massive swords belonging to Mehmet Fatih and the earlier Sultans. These are not only large, but impressive even inside a display case.

The swords of the later Sultans, however, become increasingly smaller till they are obviously just jewel encrusted ceremonial daggers that look incapable of peeling an apple. The disparity between the earlier and latter periods is silent evidence of the decline in military power of the Muslim world.

Tower of Justice:

The Sunset of Justice

The original purpose of this structure was to provide a direct link between the Harem and the Imperial Council chamber. It was also for the Sultan to keep a watch over his ministers and to ensure that injustice did not take place. The high vantage point by the tower also allowed the Sultan to keep a watchful eye over his city.

Eventually, the Sultan no longer attended most cabinet meetings of his ministers, so the tower was mainly used to merely symbolise the watchful eye of the Sultan over government. Finally, the government, including the Grand Vizier, were relocated to a separate building outside the palace. The tower was now only used as a secluded vantage point to see the city.

From the Tower of *ensuring* Justice to the Tower of *assuring* Justice – without ensuring it at all – and finally dropping the pretence altogether. The fate of the tower mirrors how the Empire went from a strict meritocracy with the rule of law, to a byword for oriental corruption over the course of several centuries.

Bab-us Saadet (The Gate of Felicity):

The Standard of the Eagle

This is an exclusive gate of the entire Palace. Beyond this, only the highest officials in the land could go through – but sometimes even they would be denied entry. It was outside this gate that the Ottoman throne would be placed after the coronation of the new Sultan at the Masjid of Eyüp Sultan. There are existing videos of the last Sultan, Mehmed Vahideddin, receiving the oath of allegiance of his subjects whilst sitting on the throne at this gate.

However, the unique feature of this gate is not the Ottoman throne or the exclusive access, but the small stone on the ground cordoned off by velvet ropes. At times of extreme distress or importance, the flag of the Prophet ﷺ would be taken out and affixed to a standard attached to the stone.

The Prophet's flag was called "Al-Uqab" – the Eagle. Muslims took great care not to fly it except on very special occasions, but legend has it that no battle was ever lost when the Eagle flew. It must have been an awe-inspiring sight to see it unfurled once every few generations and to witness the impact it had on all present.

Though there is a marker and security ropes preventing anyone from walking over the stone in which the Prophetic flag would be fixed, there is no such marker or protection for the location of the Sultan's throne. It is a small indicator perhaps that Sultans come and go, but the Mercy to the Worlds' ﷺ glory transcends that of even the greatest rulers.

Arz Odasi (Audience Chamber):
The Heart of the Empire

During the Ottoman Empire, if you were looking at this room, then you knew you had made it. Only the most important people in the world would be allowed to enter the gate and into this room.

Even the Grand Vizier had to ask permission to enter. The Council Chamber – that you would have already passed in the second courtyard – was where the official meetings were held. This was where the Sultan would have his more intimate post-meeting meeting with a smaller group of people. This was akin to the Oval office of the Ottoman Empire.

The Audience Chamber was deliberately placed to block the view of the courtyard since that courtyard was considered the Sultan's private home. As Viziers and Ambassadors from other countries could be admitted to the Arz Odasi, it was important to situate it in a way that maintained the Sultan's household's privacy.

The grilled gate to the left of the door is where all gifts for the Sultan were placed. The water fountain to the right was installed by Sultan Suleiman the Magnificent to provide convenient drinking water if needed, but also made it harder for anyone listening at the gates to hear what was discussed inside.

The Arz Odasi is surprisingly compact with a large section taken up by the absolutely gigantic throne sofa that is larger than a King size bed. The intimidating effect it would have on visiting dignitaries can be imagined with those allowed an audience with the Sultan. You were lucky enough to be granted an audience, but you were left in no doubt as to who was in charge.

The Treasury:

The Fleeting Nature of Wealth

This may be the closest you will ever get to entering Ali Baba's Cave of Wonders from the Arabian Nights. The Treasury was a storeroom of treasures that many had dreamt of, but extremely few had ever seen with the priceless objects of many lands and Empires deposited here. There are thrones from the eras of various Sultans, a golden cot, priceless paintings and kaftans. The world famous Topkapı dagger immortalised in the movie *Topkapı* is also on display. And of course, the treasury contains the usual suspects of gold, emeralds, rubies and everything in between. However, it also contains some treasures that are truly priceless.

We would imagine that the Sultan would have spent a great deal of time in this room counting and admiring his wealth. This was not the case. Each Ottoman Sultan was expected to visit the treasury when they ascended to the throne, but very few came back after that. These halls full of wealth, each box of which contains more than the average person could earn in a lifetime are a reminder of the fleeting nature of worldly wealth. Acquired over lifetimes and centuries yet here they are, while their masters lay buried under the ground.

When Sultan Ahmed I visited the treasury after becoming the Sultan at a very young age, he ordered the largest diamonds in the treasury to be sent to Madinah and clipped onto the covering of the Prophet ﷺ's tomb instead. It was eventually returned to the treasury, but it is unclear under what circumstances.

The gate of the treasury has the seal of Sultan Selim I. He affixed it there in a challenge to his successors stating that he had filled the treasury so copiously during his short reign that his seal should not be removed from the doors until one of his successors manages to fill it more than he had. In a mark of the scale of his successes, the seal of Selim I remained affixed to the gates of the Treasury till the end of the Empire.

The Treasury:

The Spoonmaker's Diamond

Long ago, a court official was walking through the Bazaars of Istanbul when he came across something that caught his eye on the stall of a man who made spoons. He asked the man what it was. "This? This is just a pretty crystal that I use as a paperweight. You can have it if you want."

Of course, the court official knew that this was no paperweight. What the man had mistaken for a paper weight was in fact the world's largest diamond – the size of a human fist. Seeing an opportunity to advance his career, he purchased it for a nominal price and then presented it to the Sultan whose eyes nearly popped out of his head when he saw it.

Tradition states that the owner of the diamond gets to name it. The Sultan was asked what he would name this magnificent diamond – the largest in the known world at the time. He replied, "The Spoonmaker's Diamond."

This name highlights the reality that we all hold incalculable wealth that others would give everything for, whether it be good health, a happy family life, security or our faith. However, only a few truly recognise their worth when it is in their possession. There is no doubt that each of the blessings we have are priceless diamonds that others who do not have can only dream of. The only question is whether we are the Spoonmaker or the Sultan?

Enderun Library:

Too Little, Too Late

The importance of education and seeking knowledge in Islam cannot be overstated. From the very first word of the Quran being "Read", to the sayings of the Prophet ﷺ exalting the ink of a scholar over the blood of a martyr – we have been encouraged, some would say ordered, to seek knowledge. Yet today, the best educational institutions are located exclusively outside the Muslim world.

The Enderun Library was the library of Sultan Ahmed III – the Sultan of the Tulip era. In keeping with his personality, he collected rare and important manuscripts into this prominent building right in the centre of the 3rd courtyard.

The Ottomans were fanatical about recording and documenting everything that happened in court, from the number of pistachios needed for the Valide Sultan's meals to the most important treaties negotiated with world powers. Today, many of the ancient and priceless manuscripts have been moved to another building on site, the Mosque of the Aghas.

Even though a few Sultans had an interest in books and education, the Ottomans it may be argued that something was lacking in promoting a culture of learning. Hundreds of years before the conquest of Constantinople, the Andalusian capital of Cordoba boasted one of the largest libraries in the world. Baghdad had the House of Wisdom; Cairo had the Al-Azhar and Fez had the Qarawiyin. Istanbul feels like it is lacking in this regard.

The Ottomans were exceptional warriors and administrators, but average scientists or artists when compared to other Muslim dynasties in Baghdad, Cordoba or Samarqand. This disconnect meant that while the rest of the world was waking up to the scientific revolution and educating the masses, the Ottomans were still far behind. It would be a fatal error that would, like the failure to adopt the Industrial Revolution centuries later, set the Muslim world back hundreds of years.

Mosque of the Aghas:

Leonardo's Lost Bridge

When Mehmet Fatih conquered Constantinople, one of the first orders of business was to build a bridge that spanned the Golden Horn. The current bridge was a string of boats tied together and this was hardly stable, let alone befitting of a world capital. The Ottomans asked for entries from across the world and these started pouring in, including from an up-and-coming architect called Leonardo Da Vinci.

Leonardo was, unfortunately, already engaged in working for another patron. By the time he had finished that assignment, Mehmet Fatih had been poisoned and his son Bayezid was on the throne. Leonardo wrote to Topkapı asking if he could still try and build the bridge.

The Ottomans had moved on, but Leonardo kept writing hoping to get the commission. A surviving note in the Ottoman archives in the mosque of the Aghas has a letter from Leonardo with a handwritten note by the Vizier who filed it stating, "Why won't this infidel leave us alone?"

Leonardo's masterpiece bridge was never built, and he had to go back to other projects like painting and sculpture. However, despite never being built, he had made detailed notes on what he wanted it to look like and soon the unmade bridge became legendary and sometimes known as the Mona Lisa of Bridges.

It is worth wondering how things would be different if Leonardo had got the job. Would the Mona Lisa have ever been painted? Would he have been sucked into Ottoman culture and even the Muslim faith? Would he have designed a grand Mosque? We'll never know the answers, but recently, a Norwegian architect went through historical records and finally constructed the bridge that Leonardo proposed to Sultan Beyazid. The bridge opened in Norway in 2001 to critical acclaim.

The Mosque of the Aghas:

The Most Precious Copy of the Quran

The Mosque of the Aghas was the personal mosque used by the Palace officials and the Sultan for the majority of the Ottoman Empire's existence. It was conveniently located and with space for the women of the harem as well. The Sultan, his slaves and even some of the humble servants of the palace would all pray in the same mosque without any distinction towards rank. There was no separate lodge or Hünkâr Mahfili here.

Today, the Mosque houses the book collection from the Enderun Library accumulated by various Sultans. Amongst all the valuable tomes and treatises is the most precious book in the Muslim world; the Uthmani Quran.

During the reign of Abu Bakr (R), the Quran was collected into a single book for the first time. This master copy was kept in the room of Hafsa (Ra) – the wife of the Prophet ﷺ and the daughter of Umar (R.) It was meticulously checked and rechecked by the many companions who had memorised at the feet of the Prophet ﷺ himself.

During the reign of Uthman (R) – six copies were made from the master copy and sent to the main centres of the growing Muslim world.

It was this copy of the Quran in Topkapı palace that is rumoured to be the version being read by Uthman (R) himself when he was assassinated – his blood spilling on to an apt verse, "And Allah will suffice you against them."

Only three of the six Uthmani Qurans are known to have survived. One is in the Hussein Mosque in Cairo, the other is in Tashkent, Uzbekistan. The final one is here in the Topkapı Palace.

Sofa-i Hümayun (The Imperial Sofa):

A Palace and a Home

Rather than keep their throne room and their family parlour separate, the Imperial Ottoman art of work-life balance was one of coexistence in the same space.

The Sofa-I Hümayun was the main audience chamber and throne room. The Ottomans did not have Western style hard thrones that were uncomfortable to sit on. Instead, they had magnificent sofas. The word itself comes from the Arabic "Suffah" which was traditionally a slightly raised area for sitting on that was often richly covered and cushioned.

There is a secret door behind one of the mirrors in this room allowing the Sultan to slip in and out as he wished. Making an unexpected entrance and exit have always been part of producing a royal aura.

This was not just the throne room but also the family living room with Iftars, Eid celebrations and even family weddings all taking place here with the male members of the family in the main hall and the ladies in the galleries on the side. It is interesting to note how much Topkapı combined the role of palace and family home throughout its layout.

Harem:

Introduction

In fevered imaginations, a Harem was thought of as a place of debauchery. Paintings and novels by Western artists who had never seen one, drew pictures that left an impression that lingers on even to this day. The lecherous Muslim man surrounded by women in his pleasure den is a familiar trope. Entering this area will quickly disabuse someone of that notion. This is another locus of power every bit as important as the Council chamber you just passed.

If the courtyard side entrance of the Harem makes it look like it was an afterthought to the design of the original palace, that is because it was. It seems that Mehmet Fatih wanted to keep the Old Palace (located in Beyazid square and now the site of Istanbul university) as his personal residence with Topkapı being the seat of Government. This meant that there was a strict separation between the Sultan's personal life and his role as the leader of the country.

However, during the reign of Sultan Suleiman the Magnificent and the Empress Hurrem, it would simply not do to keep the Harem so far away from the Sultan. Suleiman was too in love and Hurrem was too savvy to be left out of the loop. Eventually, the harem would have to move to Topkapı.

In the years that followed Sultan Suleiman, a series of weak Sultans were dominated by their more intelligent and capable wives, mothers and grandmothers. This was the so-called Sultanate of Women. The women of the Harem were no longer just there to fulfil the function of providing a suitable number of heirs and spares to the Sultan. They were now taking an active, even if slightly secretive, part in political life too.

The haphazard wooden structures were converted to more permanent but still haphazard rooms constantly evolving as the size – and influence – of the Harem continued to grow.

Courtyard of the Consorts and Concubines:

Not Quite What you Expected

From apartments to kitchens, laundry rooms to a small cafe, the courtyard houses what are just private living quarters for the women of the Sultan's household including his mother, sisters and daughters. The Harem seems a lot less exotic than the rest of the palace with the living space being more functional and less opulent.

In keeping with the strict seclusion that was expected of them, the women of the Harem had their own private pathways to the gardens, their own mosque and even a separate hospital. They were not purely pleasure slaves kept in dungeons or house arrest as some would have you believe. In fact, most of the women in the Harem had access to the best education, healthcare and extra-curricular activities than any other women in the Empire.

The Sultan himself did not have a bedroom here because he was expected to spend more time running the Government than with his family. This situation did not last long, and successive Sultans retreated into this small space leaving the fate of the Empire in the hands of others. The Prophet ﷺ taught us a middle path that the Sultans forgot to the detriment of their empire – and we forget to the detriment of our communities.

Favourites (Haseki) Apartments:

House of cards

Haseki Sultan was the title given to the chief consort of the Ottoman Sultan, the closest thing to a Queen. In the early days, these were few, but their number and influence grew as Sultans became ever more involved in the harem and divorced from the public sphere. Eventually, during a period known as the Sultanate of the Women, almost all pretence was dropped, and the Empire was run by a series of remarkable women from these apartments.

Today we cannot see inside them, and the area seems to be just rooms of varying sizes, but make no mistake, the location and type of apartment was a matter of life and death for those in the harem. Those who made it would secure their place and that of their children. Those who did not risked being exiled to the Old Palace and their children being executed in front of them. The harem became less a family space and more the centre of power politics that would distract Sultan after Sultan.

Courtyard of the Eunuchs:

Juristic Gymnastics Can't Hide the Truth

Eunuchs make multiple appearances throughout Ottoman history. They are always there in the background, completely loyal to their master, by turns dangerous or courageous. The Ottomans seem to have been equal opportunity employers when it came to Eunuchs as they had both black and white Eunuchs. Race, however, did play a role in what roles they would be given.

A Eunuch's worth lay not in what they had, but what they now lacked. Unable to father children, they were never going to be distracted by family. Work was their life. In addition, they were "safe" to work in the harem without their master worrying about them having an affair with the slave girls. As it turns out, this was not entirely accurate.

The act of castration itself was explicitly against Islamic law. This is not a surprise as Muslims are warned against even hitting someone in the face lest it causes any disfigurement. The Ottomans got around this by getting non-Muslim slave traders to carry out the procedure. They assuaged their conscience by saying they were simply the customers. This conveniently ignored the fact that as long as there was a market for Eunuchs in the Ottoman Empire, there would be slave traders willing to take young children and mutilate them to make a profit.

Harem:

Running Water and Blocking Secrets

As you will see, the harem is a crowded place even with the tourists that you see today. Now, imagine it with the full complement of princes, princesses, their slaves and retinues; it would be difficult to get any privacy.

One of the brilliant ways they managed to make sure that discussions were less likely to be overheard was by placing fountains and taps in windows. The sound of flowing water was both soothing and managed to obscure the whispering of those speaking inside the room.

The need to maintain secrecy lends weight to the political nature of some of the discussions taking place within the harem walls. Other techniques used to maintain secrecy included strategically planted trees and flower beds.

Imperial Baths:

Protection or prison?

Turkish baths are famous the world over for their rejuvenating and cleansing treatments, and as one of the forerunners of the modern spa. So, of course, the bath of the Sultan himself would need to be something special. If there was a pinnacle of the Hammam, then this would have to be it.

The Imperial baths do not disappoint. Designed by Sinan (is there anything this man did not design?) they were originally decorated with brilliant Iznik tiles. However, during the construction of the Blue Mosque the entire city of Iznik could not keep up with the demand for Iznik tiles. The Sultan, in a sign of how dedicated he was to his deadline, had his own bathrooms stripped of tiles and donated them to the Mosque.

The baths followed the Roman system of a series of hot baths, tepid baths and then a cold bath that would maximise cleanliness and rejuvenate the bather. Even though they were tucked deep into the heart of the palace, Sinan found a way to bathe the entire area in light whilst still maintaining the privacy of those inside.

The golden grills around the baths are in place so that when the Sultan was performing his ablutions, he was safe from any attempt at assassination. This, however, did not save Selim II from a far more insidious enemy – wet marble. He slipped and endured a likely brain haemorrhage that was fatal a few days later. It is a reminder that death can come for us, even in the most secure of locations.

Apartments of the Valide Sultan:

A Rollercoaster Ride of Power and Obscurity

The Sultans were one of the most powerful people in the world. Their word was law, and they could make or break entire countries should they wish to. There was only one person who could bring the Sultan – Commander of the Faithful, Lord of the Two Seas, the Shadow of God on Earth – to heel. It was, of course, his mother.

More than most Empires, the Ottomans institutionalised the role and respect of the matriarch to a degree that would be unthinkable before or since. It is instructive to think of the special status afforded to the mother: despite her previous position as a slave-girl or her different ethnicity, the Valide was treated with the respect and reverence that Islam demands for a mother.

The mother of the Sultan was second only to him in the hierarchy. This is reflected in the special apartments set aside for her. The apartments have a private prayer area and a tile depicting the Masjid Al Haram in Makkah – even more remarkable as very few of the Valide Sultans were ever born Muslims.

Slave girls, born non-Muslim in a strange land, would have grown up in the cut-throat atmosphere of the most elite finishing school in the world; the Harem of the Sultan. Then, upon the death of the Sultan they would be banished to the Old Palace (also known as the palace of tears) miles away, awaiting the inevitable end of all living beings.

Then suddenly one of them would find out that their son had ascended the throne and would be whisked away from the Old Palace and into their own apartment at Topkapı directly connected to that of their son, the Sultan. From slave-girl to the mother of the Sultan in a matter of moments.

The ascent is dizzying to think of, much less to experience. And yet, the most curious aspect of the most rapid promotion in history is significant in another respect: The Prophet ﷺ was asked about the signs of the Day of Judgment; one of them was that the slave girl shall give birth to her master. To many, this meant that women would give birth to children who would treat their mothers harshly. Yet, it was a precise description of the Ottoman ascensions: slave girls giving birth to a child who would immediately be higher up in the hierarchy than them.

While the figures depicting life in these apartments give a sense of what it must have been like, they can hardly convey the emotions that were contained within these walls, where power could disappear with the death of a Sultan as quickly as it had appeared with his ascension.

Apartments of the Crown Prince:

From House Arrest to the Throne

One of the most horrifying aspects of Ottoman history was the institutionalisation of fratricide. As discussed previously, this was the practice of the new Sultan having all his brothers (indeed all male members of the family) strangled to death on his ascension to the throne.

This was justified by earlier Sultans as being a lesser evil than civil war. That is debatable and although the Ottomans had fewer civil wars than most of their contemporaries, the ruthless rivalry produced an atmosphere in the harem that was less women's quarter and more death match.

Sultan Ahmed I abolished this terrible custom and instead put the Crown Prince (and others) in these apartments as virtual prisoners. In recognition of the opulence of this prison – the apartments became known as "the Golden Cage."

Unfortunately, there was a sting in the tail. Growing up in a few rooms of the palace for decades at a time, these princes became mentally deranged or at least sociopathic. They certainly were not fit to run a household, let alone an Empire. But that is the terrible thing about monarchies – it does not matter whether you are up to the job or not; all that matters is your family name. Although the Muslims' world started off as a meritocracy, it soon reverted to a monarchical system with extremely few exceptions in over 1400 years and has stayed true to this flawed model of leadership.

Privy Chamber of Murad III:

The Rise of the Sedentary Sultan

Murad III was the not-so-magnificent grandson of Sultan Suleiman. He spent much of his reign in Istanbul and was increasingly cut off from his people. In fact, for the last two years of his reign, he did not even attend Friday prayers in the Mosque. He performed all five daily prayers in the palace and secluded himself there.

This seclusion was no doubt helped by having a beautiful room like this built in the harem with large reclining areas and a beautiful fireplace. The Ayat al Kursi runs across the room in beautiful, brilliant blue tiles – perhaps to remind the Sultan that no matter how influential his throne was, it would never compare to that of the throne of the King of Kings.

When we look at these rooms, it is difficult to imagine them as they were at the time of the Sultans. It would be akin to someone visiting our own bedroom and trying to guess at how we lived based on bare walls and empty floors. We get no idea of the soft furnishings, the items of decoration that dotted the room with opulence or how the lighting played with all these ornaments.

Murad III was a contemporary of Queen Elizabeth I of England. Both shared a common enemy in the Catholic states of Europe. Sultan Murad justified his alliance with Queen Elizabeth by stating that both Protestants and Muslims were against the worship of idols, taking a dig at Catholic veneration of statues and saints.

Their alliance was not to be purely theoretical. When Spain aimed to invade Britain with their armada, the Ottomans performed naval manoeuvres in the Mediterranean. The Emperor of Spain had to split some of his fleet between the Armada invading Britain and defending their rear against the Ottomans. This brought the English valuable time and, eventually, victory. There are many who see the modern influx of Muslims into Europe as a threat to their way of life, forgetting that we, often, played a constructive role instead.

Privy Chambers of Ahmed I and Ahmed III:

Even a Sultan needs to Disconnect

As anyone who is serious about getting some work done will attest to, having a study is a major benefit. The Ottoman harem could be a distracting place. For the pious Ahmed I, this privy chamber, complete with bookshelves, tables and a lectern for his Quran, was the perfect location to step away from the distractions on his time.

Contemplation has great value in Islam. Even the home of Khadijah (RA) in Makkah, the home that the Prophet ﷺ spent the longest period of time in, there was a room reserved just for the Prophet ﷺ. Being able to spend time reading, writing and thinking is considered a luxury in this day and age where it is easy to get caught up in the never-ending tasks that make up our existence. Yet carving out a space and some time for personal development and reflection is as important today as it was before – as Sultan Ahmed clearly knew.

The small privy chamber of Ahmed III is unique in the palace in terms of its decoration and paintings. It was built by the flamboyant and rather unique Ahmed III (the Sultan of the Tulip Era.) The creation of this smaller private privy chamber shows that even the Sultans desired to have some space to relax and be alone in the harem. It is a feeling that we may be familiar with in our interconnected times.

It is thought that the chamber served as the private dining area of the Sultans for when they wanted to eat away from the noise of the harem. It was just the kind of thing for a contemplative and artistic Sultan. The depictions of fruit reflect their special significance in Islam, namely their mention in the Quran. Indeed, a description of Paradise reads, "therein for them is every kind of fruit."

Chamber of Sacred Relics:

Location of Sacred Relics Room

This series of rooms was the earliest location of the throne room and the Sultan's private bedroom. Since the sacred relics were beyond the status of treasures, the safest and most honoured place to keep it would be where the Sultan resided himself.

The throne room is off limits, but you can look in via the threshold and view the throne as well as the case that holds the mantle of the Prophet ﷺ. Just outside the room is the base of a pillar. The hollowed-out section was used for mixing ingredients to make the special incense that provided a pleasant fragrance. It was one of the most exclusive fragrances in the world, the ingredients included the dust collected from cleaning the Prophetic chamber.

The calligraphy over the door states the testimony of faith: "There is no God but Allah and Muhammad is His messenger." This was personally written by Sultan Ahmed III. You are not allowed to take pictures here, but perhaps that is a good thing; some things are meant to be experienced by the soul and not just by the eyes.

Chamber of Sacred Relics:

Provenance

When the last Abbasid, Al Mutawakkil III, handed over the authority of his office to Selim, he also handed over the symbols of it too. These included sacred relics from the earliest days of Islam.

These days, it is easy to be sceptical about many of these items, but that would be a mistake. While poor curating has meant that items of varying authenticity are displayed together, the items related to the Prophet ﷺ have the best provenance of any such relics around.

For example, it is known that certain strands of hair of the Prophet ﷺ were kept by companions and eventually these hairs passed on to either institutions or were collected by the ruler himself. The Umayyads collected many of these objects and from them it passed to the Abbasids and from them to the Ottomans.

For some, the lack of hard catalogued evidence of the provenance for the Prophetic relics means that they are immediately suspect. This does not consider the complexities inherent in verifying and authenticating historical objects – even with modern technology. Our faith is not dependent on any relics and therefore their authenticity or lack of is only as important as the amount they connect us to our heritage.

Chamber of Sacred Relics:

Yavus Selim: Conquest of Egypt and Hijaz

There is a tipping point for Empires: it is a point from which you suddenly break away from the pack and you look around and there is no one else that can touch you. For the Ottomans, this point came just after their conquest of Mamluk Egypt.

Yavus Sultan Selim had just received the Abbasid Caliph Al-Mutawakkil III into his presence. After the latter had pledged his allegiance to the former, Al-Mutawakkil did something that none of his predecessors had ever done. He handed over the title and the symbols of caliphal authority to the Ottoman Sultan.

There are some modern-day historians who argue that this event never happened. They do their best to declare that no such transfer of Caliphal authority took place, that the office simply disappeared into the ether, that the Ottomans never claimed the office and it was only mentioned centuries later as a counter to the Russian claims to protect the Christians in Ottoman territories. Each one of these claims is patently absurd and more a reflection of a desire to delegitimise the Ottomans rather than based in fact.

Whether the transfer of power was done under duress or willingly is not recorded although it matters little since transfers of power are rarely voluntary. In either case, at the Friday prayer sermon, the Imam made dua'a for Selim. It was a momentous event in the history of Islam.

There could be no greater indication of how momentous a moment it was than to note that when the Imam called him the "Ruler of the Holy Cities" the stern and grim Selim poured soil on his own head (in a sign of humility) and corrected him saying, "Servant of the Holy Cities." As went Cairo, so went the rest of the Mamluk lands, including the Hijaz. Till this day, the ruler of Makkah and Madinah is called the servant of the two Harams.

Chamber of Sacred Relics:

The most exclusive event in the world

On the 15th night of Ramadan, the most exclusive event in the Ottoman calendar would take place. A few dozen individuals of the highest rank would gather outside the threshold of the chamber of sacred relics. They had been personally invited with a hand-written letter from the Sultan. Today we get to see it for the price of a ticket.

The Sultan would enter the Chamber of Sacred Relics first and start cleaning the rooms. After some time, the others would be admitted in and together, they would pray the Taraweeh prayers surrounded by these magnificent objects. Then, each guest would be given a handkerchief that had been rubbed over the holy mantle as a keepsake. Some would be allowed to drink from the water the handkerchief was cleaned in.

To be invited to attend this event was a real honour not even given to most of the ruling family. It was a chance for these individuals to connect with our heritage in a meaningful way and to observe treasures that cannot be defined. Today we get to see it for the price of a ticket.

Chamber of Sacred Relics:

Hair of the Prophet

Having witnessed the Prophet ﷺ during his lifetime was such a high honour that it literally differentiates between the generation that can call themselves Companions and those who cannot.

After his ﷺ death, it is only the lucky few who saw him in a dream that were able to share in that honour – even if in the most ephemeral sense. In the history books, it is a rare privilege mostly bestowed on the most pious and legendary of us. And yet, for the price of a flight to Istanbul and entry to the Topkapı Palace, you can gaze at a hair from the head of the greatest man to have walked the Earth.

The hair itself is a memento of the man who had had a greater impact on our lives than even our own parents. It is a physical reminder that Muhammad ibn Abdullah ﷺ isn't just a figure from the Seerah or history books but was a real person who was given a job that was not bound by time or space, even though his earthly existence was.

Chamber of Sacred Relics:

The Prophet's Tooth

Every society celebrates their greatest victories, but it is rare to commemorate the defeats. The battle of Uhud was one such moment of Islamic history. The battle came hot on the heels of the Battle of Badr, where the young Muslim community of Madinah crushed their arch-rivals – the powerful and wealthy Quraish.

The battle of Uhud started off in the same vein, the Muslims having the upper hand and pushing back the Quraish with ease. However, at the moment of victory, the archers posted by the Prophet ﷺ to guard the rear side, began to lose their discipline. Thinking that the outcome was now a foregone conclusion, they left an opening for a brilliant young man who was watching like a hawk for just such a moment.

Soon, victory turned into defeat with Khalid ibn Walid and his cavalry attacking the Muslims from behind and thereby causing the main Muslim army to be trapped in a pincer movement. In the commotion, an archer from the Quraish army decided to use the opportunity to assassinate the Prophet ﷺ himself. The Prophet ﷺ was struck on the side of his face by the arrow.

The chain armour that was protecting the Prophet ﷺ became embedded in his cheek and two of the Prophet's teeth fell out. They were buried with due care while the Prophet ﷺ was evacuated to safer ground.

At the fall of Madinah during World War I, one of the objects dug up and transported secretly to Topkapı was the tooth or teeth of the Prophet ﷺ. It was feared that leaving it in place would mean that the teeth would be discarded or lost.

Today, you can be just inches away from part of the Prophet ﷺ himself and the most dramatic reminder that even the greatest of all creation suffered when we become disunited.

Chamber of Sacred Relics:
Kaab and a Very Special Poem

There were not many fields that the Arabs could claim superiority over others in before the advent of Islam, but there was one. This field came naturally to these Bedouins traversing vast expanses all alone: poetry. Amongst the most celebrated of all poets was Kaab ibn Zuhayr.

There was just one problem: he hated Islam. His hatred only grew when his brother became a Muslim, and it spilled out into poetry. Just as it seemed that he would be coming into direct confrontation with the Muslim community, Kaab became a Muslim.

He turned up in Madinah, professed his faith and then revealed his identity. Now, the silver tongue of Kaab praised the Prophet ﷺ and the faith he had adopted.

He once recited a couplet, "There is no doubt that the Messenger of God is a light, he shows us the path that is right, he is the sword of God unsheathed, to eliminate the evil that man has bequeathed." On hearing this masterpiece, in a spontaneous show of his appreciation, the Prophet ﷺ immediately took off his mantle and placed it on Kaab. This is the same mantle contained in the golden box in the Chamber of Sacred Relics.

The mantle that Kaab ibn Zuhayr received from the Prophet ﷺ was the envy of many people. Not least of these was Muawiya (R) who asked to buy it. Kaab declined, but after he passed away Muawiya purchased it from Kaab's children.

It was kept in the Umayyad treasury until the rise of the Abbasids after which it was transferred to their treasury. The mantle was preserved during the fall of Baghdad and along with a few other valued objects, it was sent to Cairo to be safeguarded by the Mamluk Sultanate.

After the fall of Cairo, the treasury was transferred to the Ottomans and the mantle went to Istanbul where it would reside in the Sultan's own apartments of Topkapı. The black mantle remains covered in seven veils and placed inside two golden boxes. In a Palace surrounded by all the material wealth of the Empire, from jewel encrusted daggers to beds made of solid gold, the most valuable object of veneration is the mantle of a shepherd from Makkah ﷺ.

Chamber of Sacred Relics:

The Sword of Khalid ibn Walid

Khalid ibn Walid (R) was one of the greatest generals to have ever lived and his exploits are so legendary that if we were to discuss them even in the most superficial way, it would scarcely be believable. He led a vastly under-equipped, inexperienced and undermanned group of Bedouins to defeat not one, but two superpowers.

In the chamber of sacred relics, it is awe inspiring to think that what we find is the sword of the Sword of Allah. Khalid ibn Walid (R) had many swords, not just one. Indeed, in one battle he went through at least half a dozen. Still, this sword connects this almost mythical figure to our own reality. The sword that stands in the Chamber of Sacred Relics is made of metal and steel. Similarly, there are swords belonging to the Prophet ﷺ himself and that of the other great Sahaaba are present too.

They are covered with designs and precious jewels now, but their value does not come from them intrinsically or from the emeralds or rubies on them but from their connection to the giants who wielded them. They were instruments in the hands of legends who set in motion events that would lead to us being Muslim today.

Chamber of Sacred Relics:

The Hand of Yahya (A)

This is an interesting exhibit. It was in the ownership of the Byzantine Emperor before the conquest of Constantinople. Although Yahya (A) is a known Prophet of Islam – there is no evidence that this arm belongs to him. According to Islamic texts, the bodies of Prophets are not decayed by the Earth and that certainly goes against the visible signs of decay on this hand.

In fact, the Ottoman Sultans likely never felt that this was authentic either as evidenced by the fact that they did not keep this relic in the chamber of sacred relics but in the treasury. Another sign is that Sultan Bayezid used this as a bargaining chip with the knights of Malta, something he would not do if he thought it was a genuine artefact. Nonetheless, when you mix up the inauthentic with the authentic, the veracity of everything comes into question; an issue that future research could potentially clarify in the Chamber of Relics.

Chamber of Sacred Relics:

Letters written by the Prophet to Rulers

Today, the Prophet Muhammad ﷺ is the model for our lives, but during his lifetime, he was an unknown Arab to all the rulers of the world. And yet, this did not stop the Prophet ﷺ from writing letters to these leaders not as a lower leader but as their moral superior – without a trace of arrogance. These letters provide us a template of how to interact with others in a way that is both polite and principled.

An actual letter dictated by the Prophet ﷺ can be found in the Chamber of Relics. The letter itself has darkened and decayed along the edges but its impact still lives with us today. The letter to Muqawqis, the ruler of Egypt, was received with respect and he sent along Maria Qibtia as a gift – who embraced Islam and bore the Prophet ﷺ his third and final son, Ibrahim.

The letter to Chosroes, the Persian Emperor, was arrogantly torn up. The Prophet ﷺ predicted that the Persian Empire would be similarly torn up within years, which turned out to be an accurate description of subsequent events.

There have been scholarly studies of these letters with debate to their authenticity. Some believe them to be forgeries created by French orientalists keen to get a big payoff from the Ottoman sultan. Others believe that the Arabic writing style and content cleaves too closely to the earliest description of such letters to be a forgery. Whatever the case, there is no doubt as to the consequences of those letters.

Chamber of Sacred Relics:

Artefacts from the Haramayn

What do you do with an important item at the Holy Mosques in Makkah and Madinah that needs to be replaced? There is no recycling centre for these priceless artefacts, and they cannot simply be discarded. Since the Ottomans ruled the Holy cities for hundreds of years, they would send all replaced material to Topkapı palace. Here, in the chamber of sacred relics, a replaced waterspout from the Kaaba would be placed alongside an old covering from the tomb of the Prophet (SAW.) Doors of the Kaaba along with their keys would be found here along with other items.

In fact, in a mark of how much reverence the Ottomans had for the Holy places, even the dust swept up from the Hujra of the Prophet ﷺ was not thrown away but placed in bottles and transported back to Istanbul along with the old brooms used for this purpose. Nothing was thrown away.

Thanks to this attitude, the Chamber of Sacred relics acts as one of the most comprehensive museums of the Holy mosques allowing a view on how things have changed and to appreciate the simplicity of previous iterations.

Chamber of Sacred Relics:

The throne and the washing table

When Mehmed VI, the last Ottoman Sultan, ascended the throne, he received the oath of allegiance of his people in front of the Gate of Felicity. After the ceremony was over, the new Sultan went inside towards the Chamber of Sacred Relics. There, on the washing table, was the shrouded body of his brother, the previous Sultan.

The Chamber of the Sacred Relics was not just a precious bedroom and throne room of the Sultans, and it was not just the reliquary of the greatest treasures of the Muslim world. The sideboard of stone that you see here is also the washing table for the ghusl (ritual bath) of deceased Sultans.

After making dua'a for the soul of his brother, Mehmed VI walked out looking sad and melancholic. He was heard to say words that were both literally and metaphorically true, "truly the distance between the throne and the washing table is very short."

Yerevan and Baghdad kiosk:

Trophy rooms

When Murad IV came to the throne, he broke the mould in more ways than one. A giant bear of a man, Murad IV was so full of contradictions as to make heads spin. Sometimes he would do so literally as he was known to be fond of beheading those he was upset with. The son of the pious Ahmed I and the formidable Kosem, Murad IV came to the throne at the age of 11 and was constantly under the control of others. Whether this upbringing made him rebel and grow up to be the fearsome Sultan that he later turned out to be, is hard to decipher.

He would punish drinking alcohol, coffee and tea by death, and he seemed to relish in carrying out executions personally on his incognito rounds of the capital. Despite this, it was said that he was an alcoholic himself, although sources are unclear as to whether these are malicious rumours or if he gave it up eventually.

His energies were not just spent on instilling fear in his subjects. He also decided that it was time to personally lead the Ottoman armies into battle once more. He successfully led the army into battle against the Safavid Empire and managed to take Azerbaijan and eventually Yerevan (today the Armenian capital.)

A few years later, he achieved his crowning achievement; Baghdad. This city held a special place in Muslim hearts as the ancient capital of the Abbasids. Although by now it was a town much reduced and still smouldering from sacks by Hulagu and then Timur, capturing Baghdad was more than just another city. It was the Ottomans declaring that they were the heirs of the Abbasids. Now, every previous seat of the Caliphate was under their control.

Each of these conquests were celebrated by a beautiful Kiosk replete with stunning Iznik tiles and sumptuous sofas. So, as you walk around them today, it is worthwhile appreciating the giant personality and stunning victories that they were made to celebrate.

Iftar Pavilion:

Take your seat at an Ottoman Iftar

Ramadan is a special time for any Muslim family and the Ottomans were no different. The beautiful Iftar pavilion is distinctive from all other pavilions as it is not designed for seclusion and privacy. This is because, unlike normal meals, which the Sultan rarely ate with anyone even from his own family let alone the common public, Iftars were enjoyed with the palace servants and the Sultan all gathered together.

The Iftar pavilion was enjoyed when Ramadan fell in the long summer months and allowed the Sultan to enjoy the view as well as the company and food. Records indicate that planning for Ramadan would start a year in advance with decorations being set up at least a few weeks before.

The atmosphere in the palace was one of such concentration and focus on the Quran that one princess likened it to that of a religious order or that of a mosque. Preparations also included the elimination of un-Islamic practices; alcohol being changed to sherbet and non-Muslim ambassadors being denied entry into the palace. The food prepared in the Royal Kitchens would not be just for the Sultan and his family but for palace staff and enough made for members of the general public.

After the Iftar, the Sultan and his court would sit and listen to Islamic lectures primarily focused on the Quran and good governance. Lessons in leadership would be shared based on the Hadith of the Prophet ﷺ as a way of warning a sitting Sultan.

The Taraweeh prayers would either be prayed in one of the Imperial mosques (Ayasofya being reserved for the 27th night of Ramadan) or in the palace itself. In the palace there were two types of Taraweeh prayer. There was a truncated version for those who had other duties to see to, but most including the Sultan and his family prayed the longer prayers.

Fish market gate:

A Life-or-Death Race to the Bottom

Executions were a common way that the Ottomans dealt with those who had fallen from favour. Although this was in keeping with the behaviour expected of royal families throughout the world, the Ottomans were different in their application to this most final of all punishments to the most elite of their society. If you were a vizier or a pasha, you were more likely to find your career ended by the executioner's blade than if you were a common criminal.

Sometimes though, they would give their victims a fighting chance, and if a vizier was summoned to the palace to have a sherbet (white for pardon and red for the death sentence) then they were given a chance to take part in a race for their lives.

From the moment they were given this news at the gate leading to the second courtyard, they and the head gardener (who was also the executioner) had to race toward the Fish Market gate. If the vizier reached there first, he got to live. If the executioner reached their first, then the sentence would be carried out and the unfortunate vizier would then have his body flung into the sea.

The fact that the last recorded episode took place as recently as the 1820's tells us much about the arbitrary cruelty that marked out much of the Muslim world at this stage while Europe was going through an age of enlightenment and scientific advancement with bright minds contributing towards the advancement of their civilization, rather than racing for their lives.

The Pearl Kiosk:

Where Will you Die?

Kiosks were small pavilions that the Turkish specialised in. They made so many of them that European travellers took the word and the concept back with them.

The Pearl Kiosk (İncili Köşk in Turkish) was built overlooking the shores of the Bosphorus by the Grand Vizier Sinan Pasha in 1590.

The Pearl Pavilion was the favourite location of Sultan Murat III. In a palace as beautiful as Topkapı, this was saying something. He would often spend his leisure time there. When he became unwell, he knew where he wanted to be.

He would wait for death in his beloved Pearl Kiosk. Surrounded by musicians and the beautiful architecture, it should have been a peaceful passing for the Sultan. However, a passing Ottoman ship realised that their Sultan was in the Kiosk directly facing them and decided the only proper thing to do was to salute him. The problem is that they saluted him with a volley of cannons which were so thunderous that they caused the roof of the Kiosk to collapse on to the Sultan and all the occupants.

He survived this show of loyalty, but his beloved Pearl Pavilion was damaged beyond repair. The Sultan had to be removed to pass away in another part of the Palace. There is a verse in the Quran stating, "No soul knows what it will earn for tomorrow, and no soul knows in what land it will die. Surely Allah is All-Knowing, All-Aware." Even the all-powerful Ottoman Sultan could not choose his own place of death.

Firuz Agha Mosque:

Symbol of Tolerance and Respect

This mosque, next to the Sultanahmet tram stop, is one of the oldest in Istanbul and gives us some clues to the early days and mentality of the Muslims in this city. It was built by Firuz Agha, the chief treasurer of Beyazid II.

The mosque is quite small, which reflected the fact that the majority of the city was still Greek Christian. We think of Istanbul as a Muslim city but for a long time after the conquest, the number of Muslims was still relatively few compared to other faiths.

The minaret is on the left of the qibla wall (rather than the traditional right side) because the right side of the mosque was home to mainly non-Muslims whereas the left side was mainly home to Muslims. Rather than build a minaret facing towards the non-Muslim side and disturbing them, it was felt that architectural tradition was not as important as being considerate to the neighbours of the mosque.

As is so often the case, while fiery conquests won the land, it was the considerate and beautiful morality displayed by the Muslims that won the hearts. Constantinople followed the same trajectory as other lands and eventually became majority Muslim.

The Palace of Antiochus:

The strange afterlife of St Euphemia

The early history of Christianity is filled with competing visions regarding key and often obscure aspects of the divinity of Christ and the Trinity itself. Much of these debates came to head in ecumenical councils held in the Eastern Roman Empire. Some were presided over by Constantine himself, desperately trying to bring some order to his newly adopted faith. Others were far more chaotic.

One of these was the strange events at the council of Chalcedon. Today Chalcedon roughly corresponds to the Istanbul District of Karakoy. There, during the pagan era, a young Christian woman was mauled to death by a bear for not renouncing her faith. Her name was Euphemia and before long she was hailed a Saint.

Much later, one of these ecumenical councils were held in the church that sprung up around her body, the Council of Chalcedon. In this council, the key question on the table was around the nature of Christ himself with two competing visions being presented before the assembled bishops and church elders. The first was that of Eastern Orthodox church and the other was the Monophysite (sometimes known as the Nestorian) view which sought to separate the divine and human nature of Christ.

At the critical juncture in proceedings, it was agreed that the creed for each would be written on a piece of paper and placed in the coffin of St Euphemia to let her decide. The next morning, the creed of the Eastern Orthodox church was on her chest and the creed of the Monophysites was found beneath her feet. A more unequivocal endorsement could not have been hoped for.

When Constantine moved to Constantinople, he had her body moved from Chalcedon to within the boundaries of the city. He placed her martyrium a stone's throw from his own palace. This location is now an empty park behind the Firuz Agha Mosque.

Basilica Cistern:

Fishing in your living room

Also known as the Yerbetan Saray or Yerbetan Sarnici, The Sunken Palace or Sunken Cistern is a testament to Byzantine ingenuity and the Ottoman respect for those who preceded them. Originally a large Roman basilica stood over this underground water source. Later, the basilica disappeared and only the cistern remained to provide water to the main Palace and its surrounding areas.

Constantinople had many cisterns throughout the old town. These were particularly useful for a city that was often under siege. The basilica Cistern is the largest of these cisterns and is fed from a fresh water source many miles away.

In one corner of the cistern are two pillar bases decorated with the head of Medusa. One head is upside down whilst the other is on its side. There have been many theories as to why they are here, but the true answer is still a mystery. The Ottomans preferred running water to the cisterns and therefore it became disused until it was rediscovered when European archaeologists were shocked to find some Istanbul residents fishing for bloated carp through a hole in their living room floor.

Having no use for it, the Ottomans could have filled in the cistern, but they simply covered it up and left it as it was. This respect for history and those that came before has come in useful many generations later and now is a well-preserved tourist attraction.

Cevri Kalfa Sibyan Mektebi:

The Reward for Saving the dynasty

When Sultan Mustafa IV was about to be overthrown by the army, he ordered the execution of the former Sultan Selim III and his own half-brother Mahmud II. Mustafa was gambling on the executions leaving him as the only male left in the Ottoman dynasty, thereby making it impossible for him to be overthrown without the need for wide-scale revolution.

Selim III was killed in his apartment, but when the executioners came looking for the child Mahmud II – they didn't find him. Instead, one of the maids, Cevri Kalfa, had hidden the child in some old clothes and stuffed him into the furnace of the baths. No one would look for a child in a furnace – even if it was not actually burning.

What was the result of this high stakes game of hide and seek? Mahmud II survived and appeared just as Mustafa IV was gloating about being the only Ottoman male left alive.

The loyalist army immediately arrested Mustafa IV. Mahmud was made Sultan and Mustafa eventually murdered. Mahmud never forgot about the maid who in the time of crisis had been decisive. She had saved his life when he was a baby, and he then built this school in her honour. Today, it is a sweet shop, but the interior still bears testimony to its historic past. Had Cevri Kalfa not been so quick thinking – Mahmud II would not have survived, and the course of Islamic history might have changed.

The Köprülü Complex:
Building a Legacy without Buildings

The Köprülü family were originally from Albania, which was a backwater of the Ottoman Empire at the time. Yet, this region gave the Ottoman State two of their most capable families. The first was the Köprülü family that ran the Empire in all but name for generations and the second was the Muhammad Ali family that governed Egypt and the Middle East for the final centuries of the Ottoman era.

The Köprülü family rose to the position of Grand Vizier, the highest position someone outside the Ottoman family could occupy. As Sultans became increasingly sedentary and disconnected from the affairs of state, Grand Viziers became more powerful and the true heads of government.

The scion of the family, Köprülü Mehmed took over at a time of great peril for the Empire. He immediately carried out a process of cleansing each part of the government, army and civil service he felt to be disloyal or corrupt. The frequency and widespread nature of the executions he carried out earned him the nickname "the cruel." It also led to the urban legend that his grave was designed to be open to the elements so that the rain could slightly cool the fire of hell burning him. This seems rather unkind as all historical records indicate that he did not kill innocents and his campaign had the necessary impact that meant the Empire recovered brilliantly.

His son Fazil Ahmed took over and masterminded many victories on the battlefield. His iron rule on every aspect of the government gave him his title of "the statist." Later members of the family include the adopted Kara Mustafa Pasha who was defeated at the siege of Vienna and paid with his head. The last great Köprülü Grand Vizier was Fazil Mustafa "the pious" who again reformed the state and patronised the Kadizadeli movement. This movement aimed to purify the religious practice of the Ottoman people by removing innovations and promoting only authentic teachings. Fazil Mustafa promoted them officially even with the Ottoman court giving them great power. Their aggressive tactics and sermons eventually created a counter-reaction which saw them exiled and banned from Ottoman state institutions.

127

One may wonder why such a powerful and long-lived family built so few monumental complexes apart from this relatively modest one near Sultanahmet square. When you read about their history it becomes clear though that for them, a well-functioning and prosperous Ottoman state was their monumental legacy.

Büyük Valide Han:

Sustaining the Mosques

Hans or hotels were built in order to subsidise the finances of mosques and other charitable foundations. The Ottomans always seemed concerned about ensuring that any charitable work such as a mosque or orphanage was sustainable financially in the long term.

The Büyük Valide Han was the closest thing that the Ottoman Empire had to a mega hotel. Located next to the Grand Bazaar in the heart of the city, with ample space for parking (your animals) and storage, the Büyük Valide Han was a travelling businessman's dream come true.

In later years, it was mainly used by Iranian businessmen. The Ottomans and Safavid Iran spent most of their time in direct competition with each other. Therefore, it is surprising to find this prime location being used by them not just for business purposes but also for religious observances during Ashura.

It was built by Kosem Sultan – one of the most intriguing and dominant women of the Ottoman family. Her original name was likely Anastasia. Born into a Greek family, she eventually found her way to Topkapı Palace – and into the heart of Sultan Ahmed I.

After Ahmed I died, Kosem should have gone into quiet retirement like her predecessors. Instead, she continued running many of the affairs of state for no less than six Sultans.

Although hated by those who resented her power, her charity work won the admiration of the people. Many Ottoman princesses took charity seriously, but Kosem took it to a new level. She would visit prisons and pay off the debt of the indebted, help poor girls get married, build mosques in small towns, and she would provide generously for the poor of Makkah and Madinah. The Büyük Valide Han (literally meaning "Big" or "Great" mother) is just one example of her generosity. Little wonder that when she was killed (on the orders of her daughter-in-law Turhan Hatice) – the people of Istanbul observed three days of mourning.

FATİH BELEDİYESİ

The Mosques of Divan Yolu:
The Harder you Fall

The Divan Yolu (Imperial Council Road) was the most important thoroughfare in Constantinople and Istanbul. Built by Constantine the Great, the road was officially the Regia (Royal Road) but was called the Mese (Central Road) by common people. It leads from the main gate of the city directly to the very heart of the Government.

As such, all buildings that lay on it were exclusively built at the behest of the most powerful members of the Ottoman elite and prime real estate. The end of the road leading up from the Grand Bazaar to Topkapı palace has a marker called the Milion. In Byzantine times, this was used as the dead centre of the city and from which all official measurements of distances were taken.

Of the many mosques to be found on the Divan Yolu, the Firuz Agha, Nur Osmaniye and the Köprülü mosques are discussed elsewhere. But the remaining mosques dotting the street at regular intervals are also interesting in their own right.

After the Firuz Agha Mosque and the Cevri Kalfa Mekteb and the tombs of Mahmud II you first encounter the Koca Sinan Pasha Mosque. This was built by the Ottoman governor who conquered the strategically vital regions of Yemen and Tunisia for the Ottoman state. He was as successful during peacetime as he was at war, building schools, mosques, inns, baths and mints. The fact that he was indispensable was shown by the fact that he became Grand Vizier no less than five times. His burial complex includes tombs and a boarding school for the study of Hadiths.

The Atik Ali Pasha Mosque was built by a Grand Vizier of Bosnian origin. He suppressed an Alevi rebellion but fell during the fighting.

The Çorlulu Ali Pasha Mosque was built by another Grand Vizier who came from a non-descript town near Istanbul. Born into a peasant family, he rose the ranks of the civil service and eventually became the right-hand man of the Sultan. He even married into the Ottoman family becoming a "Damat", (son-in-law). His meteoric rise came to an abrupt end not because he failed in battle, but because he failed to start enough of them. Çorlulu Ali Pasha tried to avoid war wherever possible, even when his enemies were distracted.

In a strange series of events, the King of Sweden, Charles XII, sought refuge in Ottoman lands after a disastrous defeat at the hands of the Russians. Even though Çorlulu Ali Pasha treated Charles and his soldiers with respect and gave them everything they wanted, he was not keen to start a war against Russia simply because the swashbuckling and slightly unhinged Swedish King wanted him to. Charles XII accused him of being bribed by the Russians and although no evidence was produced, the Sultan had Çorlulu Ali Pasha exiled and then executed. The resulting war did not go well for the Ottomans or Sweden.

The mosques of the Divan Yolu for disgraced or punished viziers showed that no matter how cut-throat (literally) the upper echelons of Ottoman political life was, the animosity did not extend into the after-life.

The Mosques of Divan Yolu:

Kara and Mahmud Pasha Mosques

The Kara Mustafa pasha complex was started by the powerful Grand Vizier who oversaw the humiliating defeat at the siege of Vienna. He paid for this with his head, but his son Ali Pasha finished the complex for the sake of his father's afterlife. In future years, the complex served as a refuge for victims of one of the regular fires that swept through the city.

The Mahmud Pasha Mosque is on the left outside Nurosmaniye Mosque. It is one of the oldest Mosques in the city built in 1462 in the Bursa style. Mahmud Pasha was Byzantine royalty who converted to Islam. He rose up the ranks of the Ottoman elite quickly, but he made powerful enemies including the son of Muhammad Fatih. These enemies poisoned the ears of the Sultan against him, and he was executed in 1474. His tomb and hammam complex are worth a visit for their unique decoration.

So many of the Mosques on the Divan Yolu were built by powerful Grand Viziers on their climb to the top of worldly power and riches. Yet, most of these powerful figures fell victim to the caprices of the power they sought, ending up executed and, often, entering their Mosques for the first time in their own Janaza.

Mahmud II Türbe / Tea Gardens:
The Final Resting Place of Sultans

This cemetery located on the main street of the Empire – the Divan Yolu – contains the tombs of three Ottoman Sultans and also many high-ranking dignitaries from the last century of the Empire. It was originally a garden belonging to the sister of Sultan Mahmud II, but it also happened to be his favourite spot in the city so he marked it out as his resting place. After his burial, it became a pantheon of the great and the good of the Empire with only the most exceptional people getting a chance to be buried there. It was even referred to as "the Ottoman Westminster Abbey" by the Times of London.

It contains the tombs of 3 Sultans. These are the tombs of Murad II (for whom the cemetery is named), his son Abdul-Aziz and his grandson Abdul Hamid II; three generations of Ottoman Sultans, all very different, buried next to each other. Abdul Hamid II was as traditional as his grandfather Murad II was modernising. Abdul Hamid II worked as hard as his uncle Abdul Aziz did not.

Before you get to the tomb of the Sultans, you pass by the graves of many dignitaries of the Empire. What you will notice is that the sarcophagi over their tombs give us an indication as to their professions. The mast of a ship indicates a captain or admiral, a book indicates a scribe or a scholar and swords indicate a general. In their prime, they were the unchallenged masters of all they saw, but today they are lying in this garden, beneath our feet. Their tombstones each contain pleas for the viewer to say a prayer and recite the Fatiha for the soul of the departed.

The main building contains the tomb of Sultan Murad II in the centre. He was the first modernising sultan. To the left of his tomb is that of Sultan Abdul-Aziz – also known as The Wrestler. He was a large man who was mainly interested in living the good life, hunting and rearing horses on his farm. He was also the first sultan or caliph to ever leave the Muslim world for the non-Muslim world without the aim of conquest. He even travelled to Paris and London on his visits where many of the public lined the streets to see the Sultan in the flesh.

135

On this tour of Europe, he was accompanied by his nephew and eventual successor Abdul Hamid II who is buried here next to him. It is said that when Abdul Hamid II died, although he had been under house imprisonment, the people lamented, and many people were distraught as he had been quietly supporting poor families, widows and orphans. "Who will feed us now?" they cried. "Who will look after us?" It is a cry that has echoed through many nations since the downfall of this once mighty family.

Mahmud II Türbe / Tea Gardens:
What's all the Fez about?

While enjoying some energising Turkish tea in the tea gardens it is worth reflecting on the different headgear on the headstones. Some of the older headstones or tombs have stylised stone turbans on them, but the newer ones, including those of the three sultans, were topped by a real Fez. And not just a generic Fez, but the actual Fez worn by them.

It is instructive of the importance of headgear in Muslim and Ottoman society that it would be the one personal item that would adorn their final resting place whether an unknown member of the public or the Sultan himself.

Early Ottoman society adopted the fashion for turbans widespread across the Muslim world. From the time of the Prophet ﷺ, turbans were used to signify importance, rank and even genealogy. As Muslim society became ever more advanced, turbans became larger and more intricate. This continued until the time of Suleiman the Magnificent during which turbans became so large and outlandish that it is difficult to imagine them being at all practical.

After crushing the Janissaries, Sultan Mahmud II outlawed turbans and allowed only the red Fez to be worn. Since every Fez would look like another, it prevented distinction based on class, religion or any other differentiating factor. It also helped his new army look different to the hated Janissaries they had just replaced.

The Fez – so called because it seems to have originated in the Moroccan city of the same name as well as where the distinctive red dye was to be found – became universal spreading as far afield as the Indonesian archipelago and throughout the Arab and Muslim world. It was also known as the Tarboosh in the Arab speaking world.

This all changed after Mustafa Kemal came to power and as part of his own reforms to divorce Turkish society from the Ottoman past, the Fez was banned, and men were obliged to wear hats with brims. This was a source of huge consternation to those Muslims who still had some attachment to their faith as brimmed hats prevented them from adequately performing the sijda (prostrations) during prayer and taking the hat off was undignified. Until about 100 years ago, it would be unthinkable for a Muslim man of any standing to be seen in public without a head covering. How quickly things change.

Mahmud II Türbe / Tea Gardens:
Sultan Mahmud II

Sultan Mahmud II was a transformational figure in Ottoman, Islamic and world history. You may not have heard of him, but decisions he made have influenced your life in ways you may not have even thought about.

Why did the Ottomans ditch kaftans and turbans for European clothing? When did we stop eating with our hands from a common plate while sitting on the floor and adopt the Western style of sitting at a table with cutlery? At what stage did the Muslim world stop trying to modernise its own traditions and instead take on Western traditions wholesale? Well, meet Sultan Mahmud II.

For years, successive Ottoman Emperors had tried to modernise the Empire in small incremental steps. Each time, their measures were either too little too late or too much too soon. One of the biggest counter-modernisation forces were the Janissaries.

The Janissaries were the elite of the elite Ottoman troops. They once were the most feared fighting force in the world. Now, they were more like corrupt policemen or security guards; more interested in petty gain than serving the Empire.

What was most damaging to future generations was that the Janissaries had wrapped their desire to prevent modernisation in the cloak of Islamic values. This led to the modernisation forces positioning themselves against tradition and Islamic values. The trope of modernity and Islam being mutually exclusive was born.

By the middle of his reign, Sultan Mahmud II had arranged everything precisely and then struck a blow against the Janissaries. The people rallied to their Sultan and by the end of the day, on the 15th of June 1826, the people of Istanbul were able to do what no foreign power had ever managed – exterminate the Janissary forces. Sultan Mahmud II had won his battle for modernisation, beginning the process that would change the Muslim world like never before.

سلطان عبد الحميد خان ثاني

Avènement 1876 SULTAN ABDUL HAMID KHAN II – 14/27 Avril 1909

Mahmud II Türbe / Tea Gardens:
Sultan Abdul Hamid II

Sultan Abdul Hamid II came to the throne during very difficult times for the Ottoman Empire. His uncle, Sultan Abdul Aziz, had been deposed and then suspiciously died. His older brother Murad V had also now been deposed. The Empire was surrounded by European powers each hungry to devour it.

Despite the many, many problems faced by the Empire at all levels, Abdul Hamid II managed to do something no one expected. He managed to bring order from chaos and to revive the economy. Not only this, but he found a way to balance the need to modernise without compromising significantly on the Islamic traditions of the Ottoman people. As such, he is widely considered to be the last great Sultan and Caliph.

Abdul Hamid II was an incredibly polarising figure. Armenians hated him for opposing their drive for secession. The West hated him for his alleged treatment of minorities. Nationalist Young Turks and Arabs hated him for his autocratic tendencies and promotion of pan-Islamic ideals that were diametrically opposed to their ethno-nationalism. The British, French, Germans and Russians all hated him for being a competent ruler preventing their desire to devour his Empire.

Despite all the pressures ranged against him, this master politician managed to profit from the disunity of his enemies to give breathing space for the Ottoman Empire to survive. Eventually, his luck and that of his Empire, would run out. On the 27th of April 1909, the last great Ottoman Sultan was deposed by the Young Turks. He spent the rest of his life in house imprisonment from where he watched his once mighty Empire disintegrate around him. One can only imagine what he must have been thinking as he saw all his efforts undone.

Otto Von Bismarck, the great Prussian leader (who not only built the modern Germany, but basically controlled the affairs of Europe for most of his life) once remarked, "If wisdom is 100 grams, Abdul Hamid has 90 grams, I have 5 grams of it and the remainder is owned by the other leaders and political figures." It has proved a common feature of Muslims that we are unable to realise the value of a good, pious and competent leader before our very eyes, denigrating them while they are alive, removing them when we can, and then lamenting them afterwards.

As his funeral cortege worked its way from Topkapi palace to his final resting place, many ordinary people were heard to cry out saying that he looked after the poor, their widows and orphans. "O my Sultan, where are you going leaving us here? Who will look after us now?" Since that day, there has been no one to answer that call.

Mahmud II Türbe:

The graveyard battle for the soul of Turkiye

In the courtyard of the Mahmud II tomb complex, as you walk to the main building housing the tomb of Sultan Abdul Hamid II, you will pass a grave on your right that at first is indistinguishable from the others of Ottoman luminaries. However, the man buried underneath, did more than most to undermine the life work of Sultan AbdulHamid II, even if he would disagree.

Ziya Gokalp, born Mehmed Ziya, was an Ottoman intellectual who helped lay the groundwork for Turkish Nationalism. Born in Diyarbakir, he saw the rising tide of Arab and Kurdish Nationalism and was convinced the only way forward was to build a Turkish version.

This he did with great success and, in no small part due to his efforts, the Ottoman Empire was heading on a trajectory that would lead to revolts and dissolution.

Some will say he cannot be blamed for this. After all, the whole world was turning towards Nationalism and away from the age of Empires. Perhaps, but there was an alternative on the table – an alternative he helped strangle while still in its infancy.

This alternative was Pan-Islamism and was championed by none other than Sultan AbdulHamid II himself. Pan-Islamism was the vision that all Muslims, whatever their background, had more in common than they had differences. It promoted the idea of Muslim unity, solidarity and integrity regardless of ethnicity, colour or background. As such, it was diametrically opposed to Nationalism.

In this life, the outcome was clear. Ziya was lauded, followed and ultimately his vision led to the founding of the modern Turkish republic. Meanwhile Sultan AbdulHamid II was deposed, imprisoned and defeated and even today the vision of Pan-Islamism is seen as dangerous. But one suspects that the outcome in this graveyard may be far different.

Cemberlitas:

The Burnt Column of Treasures

Walking between Sultanahmet and the Grand Bazaar, it is easy to ignore the large, disfigured column at Cemberlitas. It looks like just another old pillar in an area replete with them in various stages of disfigurement.

However, this column must have been something special as the entire area is named after it. Cemberlitas is Turkish for "hooped stone" which seems fitting for a column that seems to be held together by fix-it jobs of varying levels of proficiency. So, what is so special about this column?

It was originally a column that predated even the founding of the city under Constantine. When it was just another Roman outpost, Byzantium had a large pillar built honouring Apollo or Helios. The pillar itself was made of Porphyry, a purple stone that was associated with Emperors since purple was the royal colour of Rome. Emperors were clothed in purple robes and princes were "born to the purple."

When Constantine took the city, the attribution of the statue was changed to himself. However, as he was now a Christian Emperor, legends began to spring up around the column. The legends multiplied, as they often do, and before long everything from the fragment of true cross to the Palladium of Rome was said to be found at the base of the column.

Later on, the statue fell (or was removed) and replaced by a Byzantine Cross, but it was removed after the Ottoman Conquest leaving only the column, the legends and the memory of three Empires long gone.

Nuruosmaniye Mosque:

Between Worlds

From the semi-circular courtyard to the single black and gold calligraphic band encircling the inner prayer hall, the Nuruosmaniye departs from the norm and gives a spiritual atmosphere for peaceful prayer next to the chaotic hustle and bustle of the marketplace next door. This beautiful mosque located next to the grand Bazaar is unlike any other place of worship in this magnificent city.

This mosque is not just a magnificent work of art, it bristles with a palpable dual identity as it straddles two different historical periods. It bridges the space between classical Ottoman architecture and the newer Baroque architecture favoured in the 1900's. It also lies between the marketplace and the rest of the city. Finally, it was started by one brother, Sultan Mahmud I, and completed by his younger sibling, Sultan Osman III.

The architects of the Nuruosmaniye mosque seem to have embraced the transitional nature of this mosque and gone out of their way to make it unique in every way. It was said that Sultan Mahmud I wanted the building to be modelled on Baroque churches in Europe, hence the distinctive look and feel of the mosque.

The name of the mosque was kept as Nuruosmaniye (the light of Osman) after Osman III completed it, reflecting the multitude of windows allowing in natural light. The light theme is maintained by the Nur (light) verses of the Quran being used in the main interior calligraphic inscriptions.

NURUOSMANİYE KAPISI

مقام معلای خلافت اسلامیه وار یکپیرای سلطنت سنیئ عثمانیه السلطان ابن السلطان السلطان الغازی عبدالحمید

ثان غمران کستری همایونلرندن اولمق اوزره اشبو چارسوی کبیربک اوج یوز اوچ سنه هجریه یی بیع الاول ندمجددا

KAPALIÇARŞI 14
RAND BAZ

Grand Bazaar:

The Ottoman Mall

When Mehmet Fatih took control of Constantinople, it was a total ruin. This was not because of the siege that he had just put the city under but more due to the violations it suffered under the Fourth Crusade. He didn't want to destroy and pillage it like the Crusaders had done a few hundred years earlier. Instead, he wanted to return it to its former glory. In order to do that, he would need to attract people to the city. And if you want to attract people to a place there is one thing that works above all others; shopping.

Mehmet built one of the world's first and largest covered bazaars – essentially the world's first mall. He settled (sometimes by force) traders of all descriptions in different parts. There were diamond dealers, leather goods makers, carpet weavers; you name it, the Grand Bazaar had it. To this day, the Grand Bazaar is divided into sections defined by what is sold there.

Until the modern Ottoman era, it operated under a guild system where every trader belonged to a brotherhood for his particular specialty. This system ensured that prices were similar, honesty was paramount, and that standards were maintained.

The guild system promoted a way of doing business that was diametrically at odds with the capitalist mindset often found elsewhere. If someone was looking for an item, it would not be uncommon for the vendor to advise that the buyer try the shop next door. When asked why, the vendor would reply that they had already secured enough money for their family today and wanted to ensure that their brother in the next shop did so too.

Even now we see glimpses of this when we happen on a stall that is empty with the owner away. Their direct competitors in the next stall will step in and sell you the item on their behalf. It was an Islamic way of doing business that often seems to have been lost, despite the outer structure of the Grand Bazaar surviving.

The Book Bazaar:

Miscalculations and Mistakes

For bibliophiles, the Sahaflar Çarşısı (Books Bazaar) is a dream come true. Nestled between the Beyazid Mosque and the bustling marketplace of the Grand Bazaar, the Sahaflar Çarşısı provides the perfect conduit for travellers in either direction.

There is a bust in the middle of the bazaar of Ibrahim Muteferrika. He was a Hungarian revert who was the first to found a printing press in the Arabic language.

The printing press was, and still is, a sore point for the Muslim world. For an Empire so bureaucratic that they even noted down the number of note takers they had, the Ottomans were slow to adopt the mass production of the written word. They viewed it with the same scepticism that previous generations viewed the internet – unregulated and uncontrollable. It was also down to the special place books had as they were intrinsically related to our understanding of our faith.

Another complicating factor was that the printing presses were often run by non-Muslim communities like the Greek and Jewish communities. Therefore, there was a hesitation in allowing non-Muslims to control the mass printing of Islamic texts. This could have been circumvented by encouraging Muslims to get into the printing business, but agility is not a feature of a society in decline. To illustrate the point in the most damning way possible, the very first Arabic book ever printed in moveable type, was printed in the small town of Fano, Italy.

However, the accusation that the Ottomans banned the printing press and thereby leading to their decline is a far too simplistic and convenient narrative for modern day Muslim historians. This is important because if you get the wrong diagnosis at the outset, there is no hope of recovery for the patient. The Muslim world did not fail simply because of falling behind in scientific progress, even if that is a part of it.

Beyazid Mosque:

Who was "the Saint?"

Bayezid II was that rare specimen in history – a son of a great leader who was impressive in his own right. Being the son of the legendary Sultan Mehmed Fatih, "the Conqueror", he had some pretty epic shoes to fill, but if he was daunted, he did not show it.

Bayezid II was known for being even more strictly religious than his illustrious father. On ascending the throne, he ordered a review of all the laws instituted by his father. All those that were not in accordance with the Shariah were removed. His personal piety earned him the moniker of "the Saint."

His piety did not stop him from continuing the family business of conquering vast areas of the world. During his reign, the Jews and Muslims of Spain fleeing from Christian persecution and the Reconquista, were given refuge in the Ottoman Empire. He remarked about the Reconquista, "People call Ferdinand a wise ruler. Yet he has impoverished his own country and enriched mine." Not for the first time had a Muslim ruler saved the Jewish people from persecution.

Towards the end of his reign, Bayezid became disillusioned with being Sultan and the civil war between his younger sons to see who would replace him before he was even dead. His eldest son and the crown prince had given up his right to the throne as he believed that it was not possible to be a good Muslim and a Sultan at the same time. Now, Bayezid did so too and left the throne to his son Selim. He died soon afterwards.

Power is as addictive as the most powerful of drugs, possibly more so. Absolute power is even more addictive than normal; therefore, it is so difficult to find examples in history of people who have willingly let go of it. Bayezid and his eldest son did exactly that and can serve as a reminder to us that the intoxication of power does not have to overwhelm us all.

The Old palace/ Istanbul University:
The Palace of Tears

Istanbul University is the culmination of many years of evolution in education, having likely began life as a Byzantine institute of learning before Mehmet Fatih converted it into a Madrasa and a Darul funun (house of sciences.) Through many years and reorganisations, these Madrasas eventually formed the core of what would become Istanbul University.

The monumental gate that greets you is from when the area was used mainly as the Ottoman Department of War. The Ottoman government was departmentalised from quite early on, but having distinct locations for each of them was a relatively late phenomenon. The Eski Saray, the Old palace, was located on the current campus grounds.

This was the first palace built by Mehmet Fatih on conquering the city. A few years later, the court and sultan moved to the New Palace (now known as Topkapı Palace.) After this, the Old palace was used to house the harem of deceased sultans. It was thus also known as the palace of women or, owing to the melancholic situation of the inhabitants who were consigned to a life without power or freedom, as the Palace of Tears.

As you look past the gates, imagine for a second the numbers of beautiful and accomplished maidens who had to spend their entire life trapped in this gilded prison with little hope of escape or rehabilitation. The lucky few would be married off to a Pasha, but the majority would live a half-life waiting for the freedom only death can bring.

Beyazid Tower:

Watching for the Inferno

Istanbul was a city blessed with a beautiful location, but the price of this vantage point was needing to be watchful for the ever-present threat of earthquakes and fires.

Beyazid tower was constructed in the 1700's as a watchtower for the constant threat of raging fires sweeping through the city. This tower is located in the lawns of Istanbul University.

Due to the wooden houses, narrow lanes and lax fire regulations, fires were not just local events that threatened a few buildings as they are today. Fires in the past threatened to destroy the entire city. The great fire of 1660 was one such example. The fire began in a firewood depot near the centre of the city and quickly spread from neighbourhood to neighbourhood leaving hundreds of thousands homeless and many dead. More than 40,000 people were estimated to have perished.

The description of the fire still sends a shiver up the spine, with one vizier describing it as an invading army that split off into branches, each branch sent to devastate a different part of the city. Night turned into day through the intensity of the flames, and day turned into night due to the amount of ash and soot bracketing the air. By the time the fire died down 48 hours later, two thirds of Istanbul had perished.

The original tower was built from timber, which was not the smartest move, since the watchtower designed to look out for fires burnt down not once, but twice. They eventually made it of stone and came up with a system of baskets and lights to indicate whether a fire was burning and where.

Today, with less of the city susceptible to fires as houses tend not to be made of flammable material, the tower is used to signal the change in weather. The coloured lights on it indicate weather conditions – blue for clear and sunny, green for rain, yellow for fog and red for snow.

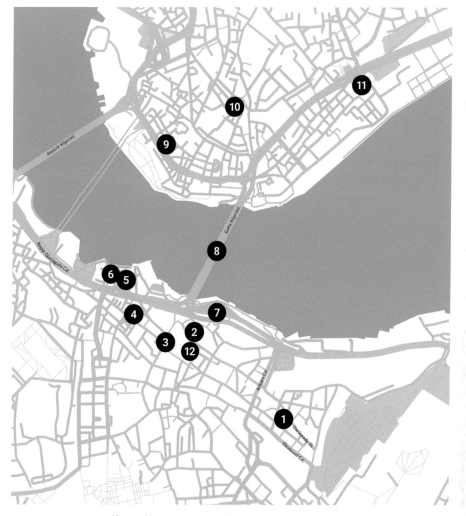

EMINÖNÜ & GALATA

1. Sirkeci Station
2. Yeni Valide Mosque
3. Spice Bazaar
4. Rustem Pasha Mosque

5. Ahi Celebi Mosque
6. Zindan Han
7. Eminonu Tram station
8. Galata Bridge

9. Arab Mosque
10. Galata Tower
11. Kilic Ali Pasha Mosque
12. Turhan Sultan Tomb

Eminönü and the Bosphorus:

The Dark Secrets Beneath the Waves

Eminönü is one of the best locations from where to enjoy the Bosphorus. The Bosphorus is one of busiest waterways in the world, with thousands of ferries transporting more than a million people back and forth daily. In addition, there are many stunning mansions dotting the edge of the Bosphorus.

The Bosphorus has always been both a blessing and curse for whoever controls it. The blessing part is easy to understand, as anyone who has had the luck to sail across its sapphire blue waters on a sunny day will attest to. The curse of the Bosphorus lies in its strategic location, controlling access to the Black Sea and the Eastern Mediterranean. As such, it has been the envy and preoccupation for capitals from London to Moscow. Whoever controlled this waterway, would gain access and dominance of large parts of the Middle East and Central Asia. It is a tempting prize.

This is also why to keep the current balance of power in the world, though the Bosphorus runs through the very heart of the Turkish nation, treaties set a century ago control who has access to it and for what purpose. A poignant reminder of the legacies of colonisation is still present throughout the world. An equally not-so-glittering discovery awaits, if one were to dive down near seraglio point where Topkapı is. There at the bottom, it is likely you would find scores of sacks weighed down with cannonballs. These were the men and mostly women who the Sultan decided to dispense with, including out of favour concubines, female thieves or rivals of the Haseki Sultan in the harem.

It is important to contextualise such behaviour to the norms of the time, but also note that such extra-judicial behaviour is a sign of an Empire in decline rather than one in ascendancy.

HISTORICAL ORIGINAL
ORIENT EXPRESS

HISTICKET ORIGINAL
SALE PRESS

Sirkeci Train Station:

The Train to Perdition

Train stations are usually places where hordes of commuters stare endlessly at screens checking to see if they can make it to home or work on time. They are not usually places of historical significance, even if a commuter might feel like they have spent a lifetime there.

Then again not many stations have the distinction of being witness to one of the most dramatic scenes in history. On the night of March the 4th, the last Caliph Abdul Majid II was given an ultimatum – either he leaves Istanbul before Fajr or else be killed along with his entire family.

There was only one way to leave the Ottoman Empire in a hurry and that was by train. After initially resisting, Abdul Majid II found himself at Sirkeci train station waiting for the Orient Express. An envelope containing £2000 in his coat pocket.

While he and the remainder of his family huddled in the cold at the station, the Jewish station master woke up and found the illustrious guests. He asked them all to come into his house that was nearby and served them some tea and snacks while they waited.

As they got up to leave and catch the train, the Caliph thanked the station master for his kindness. The station master began to cry, "You are thanking me? When my people were being persecuted across Europe, it was your ancestors that gave us refuge and saved us from extinction. It is my greatest honour that I am able to serve you in your time of need."

There was not a dry eye in the house. But unfortunately, many of the Muslims of the Ottoman Empire did not share the same views as this Jewish stationmaster. As the Orient Express set off Abdul Majid II stared out of the window as the Turkish heartlands faded into the background and sighed. He was travelling as a refugee to the lands that his ancestors had gone as conquerors.

Yeni Mosque:

Many Mothers, One Mosque

This mosque on the picturesque Eminönü waterfront, was built by two Valide Sultans more than half a century apart. It dominates the Eminönü skyline and all those who travel on the Bosphorus cannot help but notice it.

Safiye Sultana was the mother of Sultan Mehmed III and built the mosque as a symbol of her power and influence. Although the inscription on the side of building denies any ulterior motive to the building, it is interesting to note that it was originally built in the Jewish part of Istanbul.

Safiye Sultana was a controversial figure due to her excessive spending and when her son died, the Janissaries prevented her from completing the mosque due to the enormous costs involved. It lay half-finished and in ruins, just like the reputation of its founder.

It stayed that way for many decades. Then along came the powerful but much more likeable Turhan Sultana – Valide to Sultan Mehmed IV – who was asked to complete it as a sadaqah jaariyah for Safiye Sultana which she did. Since then, the mosque has been known as the Yeni Valide Sultan Mosque or New Sultan Mother Mosque to differentiate it from the older Sultan mother – whom no one seems to have had much love for.

Hatice Turhan was a Russian girl who was captured in a raid by the marauding Tatars. Sold into the Imperial Harem, this young waif like girl proved a master of political manoeuvring. Within a few years, her son was Sultan, she was the Valide Queen and everyone else on the chessboard was a pawn. Yet, at the height of her power, she chose to do something that few of her predecessors would ever even consider. For the good of the Empire, she ceded her power to the Grand Viziers, especially the capable Köprülü pasha.

While the Grand Vizier set about reforming and strengthening the Empire, she set about improving the life of the average citizen. She built fountains, soup kitchens, fortresses at the borders, mosques and schools. She was loved by her people and when she died, they had her buried in the tomb directly behind the Mosque named after her. It is well worth a visit if only to see the tomb of one who gave away that most addictive of drugs, power, in return for the eternal gratitude of her people.

Rustem Pasha Mosque:

Size Isn't Everything

Perhaps unfairly, Rustem Pasha has always had a touch of the villain about him. Whether that is because he was complicit in the shady manoeuvres of Hurrem Sultan to remove Shehzade Mustafa from the line of succession or for other reasons, it is difficult to say.

Although he was a son-in-law of Sultan Suleiman the Magnificent, Rustem himself could never hope for his eponymous mosque to compete with any imperial mosque in sheer size and scale. He (or rather, his architect, Sinan) overcame this through an ingenious tactic. As even the most unobservant visitor can note, the Rustem Pasha Mosque has the densest use of Iznik tiles of any mosque in the capital. The effect is electrifying and unique, making this medium-to-small sized non-imperial mosque into a must-see attraction in a city full of them.

Ottoman
spice
بهارات عثمانية
Osmanlı Bahı.

Curry
بهار الكاري
..............TL

Mother in law
دواء
خلط البهارة
Kaynanalıda Bıharı

Curcuma
بهار الكركم
Zerdecal
100g. 8 TL

Turk Safran
زعفران تركي
Asps 100g. 30 TL

Chicken Spice
بهار الدجاج
Tavuk

MEATBALL
SPICE
بهارات الملحم
köfte baharah

Salade-spice
بهار السلطة
Salata Bah.

B-B-C
spice
بهار المشتاوي
Barbekü B.

Tea
شاي
36 TL

Rose Tea
100 gr. 20 TL
شاي الورد
Gül Çayı

Spice / Egyptian Bazaar:

Smells of the Past

Behind the Yeni Valide Mosque is the Spice Bazaar. In the past, spices were not just used to flavour food. They were used as medicines, drugs, perfumes, chemical preservatives and even as edible credit cards. Empires went to war over them, traders became hugely wealthy, and entire continents would be colonised to ensure a constant supply. They were the equivalent to crude oil of our time – worth starting a war over.

Due to our geopolitical location between India/ China and Europe, Muslims controlled the trade of spices. Eventually we became content with just being suppliers. By hooking themselves so completely to a single revenue stream, the financial fortunes of the Muslims were precarious. The rest of the world realised that they could just cut out the middleman and sail across the oceans to get spices from China and India directly, thereby leaving the Muslim world bankrupt and struggling to find their place in the new economic world order.

The spice bazaar was built by Valide Sultan Turhan. The rent and finances coming from the nearly 100 shops located there would finance the upkeep of the Yeni Valide Mosque found in the neighbourhood.

Ahi Celebi Mosque:

Was it all a dream after all?

Ahi Celebi treated Bayezid II and his son Yavus Selim throughout their reigns. After the death of Yavus Selim, the good doctor decided it was time for him to go on Hajj. After completing the pilgrimage, he died on his return journey. He was buried in Cairo.

Having served powerful Sultans, he died a very rich man, owning dozens of villages and institutions. He left almost all his wealth to build a madrasa in Edirne and this Mosque in Istanbul.

Some centuries later, a young court official was living a pretty average life. He was preparing for an uneventful career in the civil service, perhaps as an Imam. However, he was a restless soul and one night, he had a dream. In that dream he found himself in the Ahi Celebi Mosque, but this time it was full of luminous individuals he did not recognise. He asked the one seated next to him who he was, and he introduced himself as Saad ibn Abi Waqas (R), one of the foremost companions of the Prophet. Then he pointed out the others in the congregation.

After the prayer, he was taken to the Imam who was none other than the Prophet ﷺ and was advised by Saad to ask for his intercession (shifa'at.) The dreamer so nervous that he blurted out the word for travel (seya'hat) instead. The Prophet ﷺ smiled and replied graciously, "My intercession, my travel and my ziyarat (visitation.) May God give you health and wellbeing."

The dreamer awoke. His name was Evliya Celebi, and he had his dream interpreted by a scholar who advised him he would be a world traveller. The dream turned out to be Prophetic, for Evliya became the most widely travelled Ottoman in history, spending the next 51 years of his life traversing the world and visiting towns and villages everywhere. He recorded his memoirs in a 10-volume epic, the Seyahatname – still an epic of the Turkish language and a masterpiece of Islamic travelogues.

And it all started in this small Mosque.

Evliya Celebi:

Travels of a restless soul

Everyone has heard of Marco Polo and many Muslims will be aware of the much more widely travelled Ibn Battuta. However, relatively few outside the Turkish speaking world will have heard of the legendary Evliya Celebi. Evliya was born in a house in the Kutahya district of Istanbul. His parents worked in the Ottoman Court, entitling him to an elite education. Yet, despite having a promising career ahead of him as a hafiz of the Quran and a civil servant, he opted to indulge his love of travelling. Evliya spent 40 years experiencing different cultures and so started some fantastical stories.

However, his adventures were nearly over before they began. One day he went out with his friends who were in a celebratory mood. They went to the market where a completely naked Dervish was walking through at the same time.

Suddenly, the Dervish wheeled around and started harassing Evliya. Eventually, everyone was watching the spectacle and soon laughing at the obvious discomfort of the serious palace student. Evliya became so flustered and embarrassed that he ran home leaving his friends.

Later, that evening, Evliya was sitting nursing his bruised ego at home when news came to him. His friends had gone on from the market to a brothel and created so much commotion that the Istanbul po- lice force had caught and killed every last one of them.

As the Quran reminds us, "But it is possible that you dislike a thing which is good for you, and that you love a thing which is bad for you. And Allah knows while you know not." Evliya was saved by a twist of fate and not for the first time did he feel that Allah had preserved him where others had perished. He went on to record his travels, monsters and miracles included, in the Seyahatname – the Book of Travels.

Galata Bridge:

Walk between Worlds

Walking across this bridge has been a favourite pastime for generations. The first incarnation of the bridge was probably a Byzantine bridge, but by the time of the conquest, it had disappeared.

The conquering Ottoman army of 1457 were in need of a bridge, and they weren't going to wait for it. Instead, they moored their boats side by side and made a do-it-yourself bridge instead.

Sultan Bayezid II wanted a more permanent structure to be made, and in the process rejected the designs of a trendy young Italian architect by the name of Leonardo Da Vinci. Eventually, a bridge was constructed and has undergone many revisions. The current one was made a few decades ago and had the good sense to include pedestrian, vehicular and tram access. On top of this, there are many stores and restaurants situated on the bridge itself with the freshest fish, caught right in front of your eyes.

In the past, the bridge connected the old and mainly Muslim part of the city to the newer and mainly non-Muslim part. Travelling across the bridge was not just a matter of crossing a waterway, you were crossing into different cultures and norms. Even pre-conquest, Galata was populated by Catholics while the old city was reserved for the Orthodox residents of Byzantium. Today, when you cross over the bridge, the change in culture and aesthetic is much more subtle but still present.

Zindan Kapı & Baba Cafer Dungeon:

The Abbasid Ambassador

The Zindan gate takes its name from a prison that has stood at this location since ancient times. Much of it has been destroyed, but a key tower remains. The tower was originally built as part of the defensive sea walls, but in peace times was used to house prisoners from Constantinople.

During the reign of the Abbasid Caliph Harun Al Rashid, he sent an ambassador to the Byzantine Emperor. Little is known about Jafar except that he was soon imprisoned by the Byzantines. What the charges were, if any, and why the great Caliph did not rescue him are key pieces of information lost to posterity.

What is known is that Jafar later died in the prison and was buried within the tower. Since then, it was a rite of passage for Byzantine prisoners to curse and spit on the grave of Ambassador Jafar. This situation continued until the conquest of Constantinople.

The Ottomans used Zindan Kapı as a prison as well, but having rediscovered the grave of their fellow Muslim, the tradition took on an entirely different character. It became traditional for any prisoner who was freed in Constantinople to travel to the tomb of Ambassador Jafar and pray for his soul.

Today the surrounding area is a car park, but the tomb of Jafar still sits patiently without any visitors, believers or unbelievers, as a fitting metaphor for the current spiritual state of the world.

Galata Tower:

The First Intercontinental Flight

Every city has an iconic landmark that symbolises it more than any other. For Paris it is the Eiffel tower, for London it is Big Ben and for Istanbul it is the Galata Tower.

Originally built as The Tower of Christ by the Genoese, it was topped by a large golden cross and stood as a bastion of Catholicism opposite the home of Eastern Orthodoxy. After the conquest, the cross was removed. The tower has gone through many incarnations, including as a lookout for the frequent fires that devastated Istanbul. However, the most interesting episode in its history took place in the 1600's when it served as the launch pad for the world's first intercontinental flight.

According to the Ottoman traveller Evliya Celebi, Hezârfen Ahmed Çelebi flew from the Galata Tower to Üsküdar on the Asian side of Istanbul across the Golden Horn. It was more than a few miles away and was watched by the entire city, including Sultan Murad IV.

Hezârfen had achieved one of the most amazing feats in the history of aviation. Although Sultan Murad IV was impressed by the spectacle, he promptly and inexplicably exiled Hezârfen to North Africa proving that when innovation and progress comes up against old school power – the men with the weapons usually win.

In the Western world, by and large, innovators and scientists were celebrated and rewarded handsomely. Even exceptions like the persecution of Galileo are still remembered as a stain on history, requiring the Vatican to issue a formal apology. In the Muslim world, we went from a culture of science and learning to one of persecution and denigration. The treatment of Hezârfen and other men of science in the latter Muslim world can give one clue as to why we fell so far behind the rest of the world.

Arab Mosque:

Refuge of the World

The fall of Andalusia was a seismic event for the whole of the Muslim world. In a marker of how far it had fallen from the military heights of the first 100 years, they were able to do very little about the expulsion and eventual genocide of their coreligionists.

In a campaign that began with the Reconquista and continued right through to the Spanish Inquisition, the Muslim population of Spain was gradually turned into refugees, forced converts or worse. Most of these refugees made for the lands of North Africa. Even to this day, cities like Fez in Morocco contain sizeable Andalusian quarters for Muslims and Jews.

A few decided to venture further afield than and ended up in the Ottoman Empire. These were often, but not exclusively, the aristocratic Arab families who had less faith in the Amazigh Berber ruling class of North Africa.

In solidarity with these refugees, Sultan Bayezid II ordered that the newly appropriated Church of St Paul in Galata, be given to them. From then on, it became known as the Arab Mosque. On the outside, the building still looks like a gothic era church such as found all over Europe, but once you walk inside you are welcomed into a space that is something else entirely.

One can only imagine the feelings of the refugees who had to give up their green and verdant lands along with the majority of their possessions, to be welcomed into one of the greatest cities in the world in such a manner.

Istanbul has a proud history as the home of refugees from across the world. Whether it be Muslims escaping the Reconquista, Central Asians escaping the Communist onslaught, Anatolian farmers fleeing from Armenian gangs during the first World War or Syrian people running away from the murderous Assad regime – this mosque is a proud reminder of why Istanbul remains "the refuge of the world."

A legend sprang up much later, that a companion of the Prophet ﷺ, Maslama ibn Abdul Malik was buried in the courtyard of the church. However, the real Maslama likely never met the Prophet ﷺ as he was born a generation later. He did lead the siege of Constantinople, but the Umayyad records are clear that he did not die in the siege and was prominent in court politics for quite a few years afterwards.

Saliha Sultan Fountain:

From Tears to Posterity

Istanbul is dotted by fountains as expected in most Muslim cities. People need water to drink, but for ritual ablutions (wudhu) as well. Each fountain is an endowment by some well-off patron hoping to earn their place in heaven through charitable works for the common person. Indeed, if you were going to be charitable and you did not have the astronomical sums needed to build a mosque, then you could hardly do better than a fountain. After all, in an authentic hadith, the Prophet ﷺ himself was asked "Which charity is best?" He replied, "Providing water."

The story of this particular fountain in the Azapkapi area of Istanbul began when it was visited by the Valide Sultan many centuries ago. Rabia Gulnus was on one of her many trips around the city tending to the needs of the poor, when she noticed a poor orphan girl crying near this fountain. When she asked the little girl what made her cry, she pointed to a broken pitcher on the floor.

Rabia Sultan went to the family that employed the girl and negotiated to take over the care. Saliha, the little girl, was admitted to the harem at Topkapı and within a short space of time grew up to be an intelligent and beautiful woman.

She eventually won the heart of Sultan Mustafa II and became his wife. Years later when she too was passing through the same place in Istanbul where she was found by Rabia Sultan, the memories came flooding back. This time though, they were accompanied by tears of gratitude and joy.

To commemorate her dramatic change in circumstances, she paid for the building of a magnificent fountain at the spot. It survives to this day, a monument to charity and never forgetting where you came from.

Kılıç Ali Pasha Mosque:

Where there's a will, there's a way

Kılıç Ali Pasha started life as an Italian sailor. He was captured by the Ottoman navy and condemned to be a galley slave – where the lash was long and life expectancy short. In a mark of the character of the man, he was insulted by one of the ships captains and decided the only way he could get his revenge was to convert to Islam and then fight it out. This he did and after killing his nemesis, he stayed Muslim finding an appreciation for a faith that was more egalitarian than anything he had experienced before.

He ended up joining the Ottoman navy. There he rose up the ranks from a humble sailor to eventually become the Kaptan Pasha – Grand admiral of the entire Ottoman fleet. In a swashbuckling career, he led the navy to crushing victory after victory. He even defeated his own countrymen earning him the nickname Kılıç, "Sword."

When it finally came time for him to retire, Kılıç Ali pasha became preoccupied with trying to secure his afterlife as thoroughly as he had gone about securing his career. As the Ottoman admiral, Kılıç Ali Pasha had secured more than enough wealth.

He needed to get some land from the Government to build a large mosque complex from his own money, but there was a problem. The person who decided whether Kılıç Ali Pasha would get the land grant was the Grand vizier Rustem Pasha – and Rustem Pasha hated him. Whether this was out of jealousy of the popular admiral, or some other slight, is unclear.

Rustem Pasha rudely dismissed the request saying that he would not give him even an inch of land to build the mosque on. When Kılıç Ali Pasha remonstrated as to what he should do now, Rustem Pasha sarcastically said, "You're the admiral of the seas. Go build your mosque on the sea."

Most of us would be demoralised and defeated by this seemingly insurmountable obstacle. But not Kilic Ali Pasha. He had rubble and rocks brought in and filled up the Bosphorus to build an artificial island and connect it to the mainland through a narrow causeway. Then he built his mosque on this artificial island. And a madrasa. And a hammam. And a fountain. And eventually even his own tomb. By the time he finished, we can only imagine how much he was enjoying sticking it to Rustem.

The Kılıç Ali Pasha Mosque is not just another mosque. It is a testament to how a man with a vision and dedication to it can achieve the seemingly impossible.

Pera Palace Hotel:

The Key to an Agatha Christie Mystery

Pera is a part of Istanbul that was always home to the Christian and European minority. Now known as Beyoglu, Pera has had an atmosphere more in keeping with the latest fashion and trends from Europe. It contains the famous Istiklal Cadessi, formerly known as the Grand Rue de Pera. You will find most European embassies were located in this vicinity, so the area became full of diplomats, businessmen and, of course, spies.

One would not be far off in thinking that, during the last century of the Sultanate, more of the fate of the Empire was decided here than in the palaces of the Sultan themselves. During WW2, owing to Turkish neutrality, Pera became a hotbed for espionage between the Allies and the Nazis.

The Pera Palace Hotel was one of the grandest hotels in this area and therefore the haunt of many a European traveller wanting a touch of familiarity in this capital of Islam. It has had an impressive guest list from the first three Turkish Presidents, Mustafa Kemal, Ismet Inonu and Celal Bayar to the artistic heavyweights of Ernest Hemingway, Alfred Hitchcock and Greta Garbo.

By far the most interesting recurring visitor was Agatha Christie – one of the most prolific authors of murder mysteries. During her stays, she wrote the masterpiece Murder on the Orient Express. The exploits of Hercule Poirot and Miss Marple have entertained countless generations of fans across the world.

During a refurbishment of the room, a key was found that was said to belong to Agatha Christie. Some have postulated that this key will unlock her diary or the mystery of her 11-day disappearance of which she claimed to have no memory. What there is no mystery about is the turn of the century charm of the Pera Palace hotel and how it perfectly encapsulates a society in flux, between Sultanate and Republic.

Anadolu Hisari:

Aim for perfection

This is the oldest Ottoman structure in Istanbul. It was built by the great-grandfather of Mehmet Fatih as a fortress to help facilitate the siege of Constantinople. It was only partly able to do the job as the other side of the straits were undefended and even the largest cannons could not cover the whole of the waterway. It only became truly effective once its counterpart on the European side – the Rumeli Hisari – was completed by Mehmet Fatih.

After the conquest, this magnificent fortress became a custom house and also a military prison. Today it has been restored, but its main purpose is to serve as a reminder of the sacrifice and years of dedication it took to take Constantinople. It is instructive to see the difference in preparedness between those who came before and Mehmet Fatih. Truly, he proved the hadith "Verily, Allah loves that when any one of you does a job, he should perfect it." (Al-Bayhaqi).

Rumeli Hisari:

Consistency that wins the day

The Muslims had launched expeditions to conquer Constantinople since the early days of the Umayyad Empire. Everyone wanted to be the prophesied leader that the Prophet ﷺ himself acclaimed.

However, the Muslims fell into a depressingly stagnant pattern with these expeditions. They would besiege Constantinople during the summer, but as the weather turned cold, they would leave to come back the following year and do the same again. Pretty soon the Byzantines realised that all they needed to do was to make it through the summer months and the Muslims would leave by winter anyway.

Mehmet Fatih decided he was going to have none of this ineffective and, at times, half-hearted seasonal siege. He was going to take things seriously. He had this fortress, the Rumeli Hisari, built as a counterpart to the Anadolu Hisari, so that the siege of Constantinople could be undertaken 365 days a year no matter what the weather. He gave each vizier the responsibility to build a quarter of the fortress, thereby creating a health competition between them. The fortress was built in record time and the fulltime siege of Constantinople had begun.

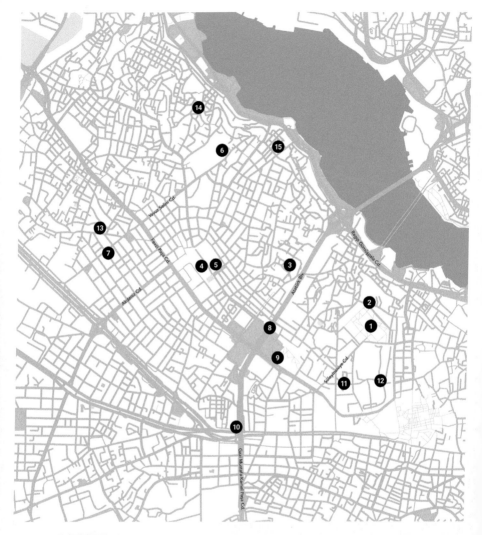

FATIH

1. Suleymaniye Mosque
2. Tomb of Mimar Sinan
3. Molla Zeyrek Mosque
4. Fatih Mosque
5. Tomb of Mehmet Fatih

6. Yavus Selim Mosque
7. Mimar Sinan Masjid
8. Aquaduct of Valens
9. Shehzade Mosque
10. Pertevniyal Valide Sultan Mosque

11. Istanbul University
12. Beyazid Tower
13. Hirke e Sherif Mosque
14. Fener Greek Orthodox Patriarchate
15. Gul Mosque

Süleymaniye Mosque

The Ottoman Empire specialised in building beautiful mosques, but there is one mosque that surpasses them all. Built on one of the major hills of Istanbul, the Süleymaniye dominates the Istanbul skyline like a sparkling sapphire surrounded by glittering diamonds. Built within an incredibly short seven-year span and with the added difficulty of being located on a sloping hillside, the Süleymaniye was a worthy monument to a magnificent century, a magnificent ruler and a magnificent architect.

You can almost imagine the spectacle of the Friday procession – known as the Selamlik – when the Sultan and his court would travel from the Topkapı palace to the Süleymaniye for Jummah prayers. The route would be lined by the public wanting to meet and petition their ruler, but also by the ambassadors of foreign nations – invited to witness (and be mesmerised by) this potent mixture of power and piety.

Suleyman occasionally called himself "the Second Suleiman" – the first being the Prophet Suleiman (A.) Although it would be disrespectful to compare anyone to a Prophet of Allah, in at least the most superficial of ways, Suleiman the Magnificent – like his namesake – was concerned with justice and built a monumental place of worship.

Süleymaniye Main Prayer Hall:
Simplicity and Power

The massive columns from Baalbek echo the magnificence of Prophet Sulaiman (A) whilst the columns from Alexandria evoke similar comparisons to Alexander the Great. Suleiman is laying claim to both the temporal and spiritual sovereignty of the world as Sultan and Caliph. You cannot help but think he is making a very good case.

One of the striking features of Ottoman mosques is that they perfect the art of understated grandeur like few others. While contemporary religious buildings in other parts of the world tried to over-awe the faithful with large statues, gargoyles and grotesques – the Ottomans went for a more minimalist look.

There are stained glass windows in the Qibla wall, red granite columns, beautiful carpets and calligraphy everywhere the eye can see – but they are not overpowering. Indeed, the Ottomans were keenly aware that the primary function of a mosque is a place of prayer and not a museum or art gallery.

This is why many architects and historians consider the Süleymaniye as the masterpiece of Sinan. To build a structure this complex and to do so by using techniques that make it look uncluttered and open is a work of genius that many fail to appreciate.

Külliye:

The Complete System

The earliest Mosques like the Masjid Nabawi in Madinah were never just a single-use building. It would serve as a community centre, a meeting place, a refuge for the dispossessed and even a prototype school or university. The Ottoman imperial mosques were often just as multifaceted in what was known as a külliye system. Külliye means complete or whole. This is where the mosque was at the centre of a range of social services and buildings for the whole community rather than just a prayer space.

The Süleymaniye Mosque was attached to a hospital, five madrasas, a medical school, a primary school, a hammam, a soup kitchen, a hospital and a hospice. This is before taking into account the unofficial buildings that sprouted up around it. This was not just somewhere you went to pray.

These other buildings provided an income for the perpetual upkeep of the mosque and its staff – just one of the reasons you would be hard pressed to find even modern mosques that are in as healthy a state of repairs as their centuries old Ottoman counterparts.

There is a more prosaic reason for the Külliye system too. It encouraged the public to see the mosque as the centre of public life. Today's Mosques are often only Musallas – prayer spaces. They have few other functions. As such, they are often seen as backward, primitive and places we must attend purely because we are required to by our faith. The Külliye were not like that. The mosque was not detached from the community but right at the heart of it – a lesson that many of today's mosque planners would do well to remember.

Suleiman I Tomb:

What made him magnificent?

Suleiman was a larger-than-life character who reigned for nearly half a century and left his imprint on the Empire.

He became Sultan on the death of his father, Sultan Selim the Grim. Suleiman continued his ancestors' work of conquering large swathes of the world. His admiral Hayrettin Barbarossa ensured that the Ottoman navy ruled the seas. The Empire expanded in all directions, ably marshalled by exceptionally talented viziers such as Ibrahim and then Rustem, only coming up short at the gates of Vienna.

Suleiman was not just a military genius. Through the hyperactive efforts of his master architect – the incomparable Sinan – Suleiman left a legacy in bricks and stone from the Ottoman porticos of the Haram in Makkah to the Süleymaniye Mosque in Istanbul. Meanwhile, his Sheikh-ul-Islam Ebusuud Effendi ensured that the theological advancements were no less striking than the military ones.

Throughout his career, Suleiman showed again and again that he was an exceptional ruler and had the good fortune of being surrounded by exceptional people. This is not just by accident though. Such talent is always latent in a community, but they need the right environment and systems to be able to flourish. The Ottomans provided just such an environment by promoting justice as the primary concern of the Empire.

This is one reason why to others he is known as Sultan Suleiman the Magnificent, but to the Turks themselves he is known as Sultan Suleiman Kanuni – the Lawgiver. Magnificence comes and goes, benefitting only those who experience it first hand, but justice envelopes everyone in the nation down to the flora and fauna.

Hurrem Sultan Tomb:
The First Ottoman Queen

Roxelana began life as a captured slave girl and ended it being one of the most powerful women in the world. Calling her life, a rags to riches story does not even begin to encapsulate what she went through.

The life of Roxelana is filled with intrigue, betrayal and murder and a genuine love story thrown in for good measure. The love of her life was none other than Sultan Suleiman the Magnificent. No one under- stood what had come over Suleiman especially as Roxelana was not particularly beautiful or exceptional. Suleiman eventually gave up all his other concubines and married Roxelana – renaming her Hurrem Sultan.

Hurrem bore Suleiman many children, but she knew that if the son of a rival was to ascend the throne, her children would be executed due to the inhumane fratricidal laws. Therefore, she worked relentlessly to remove all those who would stand in the way of one of her sons taking the throne, eventually eliminating the Grand Vizier and best friend of Suleiman, Ibrahim Pasha, and even the Crown Prince Mustafa.

Hurrem also used her powerful position to do much good and charity including providing for poor pilgrims and rebuilding the waterways of Zubayda (the wife of the even more magnificent Harun Al Rashid). However, her main legacy would be the absolute devotion she inspired in her husband. Behind every great man is a woman, but in Sultan Suleiman's case, his wife was not behind, but beside him till the day she died.

Mimar Sinan Tomb:

The Master

There are some individuals who are just so good at their job, that they not only transform their entire field, but the world with it. Think Leonardo Da Vinci and art, William Shakespeare and playwriting or even Steve Jobs and computing. In a similar stratospheric vein, Mimar Sinan was perhaps one of the greatest architects of all time.

Born into a non-Muslim family, Sinan rose through the ranks of the Janissary schools where he cut his teeth studying carpentry, mathematics and fighting in the army. He then found himself enrolled into the architecture school where his destiny awaited.

Sinan was blessed with a long life, and he used it well. Each of his buildings managed to look distinctive from each other while still being unmistakably the works of the master. Harmony between the exterior grandeur and interior comfort was key, especially when designing buildings whose main purpose was for prayer and contemplation.

By the time he died at the age of nearly 100, he had built well over 350 mosques, madrasas, hospitals, tombs and palaces. Everything from the Ottoman porticos in Makkah to almost the entire visible skyline of Istanbul, owe their existence to his ground-breaking work. Even though, out of humility, he only ever put his name to one of his hundreds of works (a nondescript bridge) they all stand as a legacy that still impacts us to this day. The Muslim world would never look the same again.

Sinan's Tomb:

The greatest masterpiece of the master

At the time of the construction of the Süleymaniye mosque, Sinan was given some land at the edge of the complex. He decided that this was to be used for his own tomb when the time came.

If you are expecting something monumental, as befitted one of the greatest architects in human history, you will be disappointed. Around the corner from a large fountain is a grilled window set into the wall that runs the length of the street. When you peer through it, you will see a plain grave not unlike any that you would find in any graveyard in Türkiye. Only a small plaque indicates that you stand before the final resting place of the master.

It is easy to be underwhelmed especially as he had personally designed his gravesite while at the height of his powers and wealth, yet instead of building a masterpiece, he went for something whose only redeeming feature is how plain it is.

However, to think like this is to misunderstand the true extent of the genius of Sinan. The Prophet ﷺ had said that the best form of charity was to "provide drinking water." This was not just the logical answer from someone living in the arid climate of Makkah, but more reflective of the fact that water is the most urgent necessity needed for the continuation of life.

Sinan could have built himself an elaborate tomb, but that would be to prioritise the structure over the purpose. Not only was it an Islamic prohibition to build elaborate tombs, but they would benefit him nothing in the afterlife. Instead, he decided to dedicate the major portion of the land to the large drinking fountain. This would serve as a form of sadaqah jaariyah (perpetual charity.)

Although most modern historians believe that the Selimiye mosque in Edirne is the masterpiece of Sinan's career, I humbly disagree. He illustrated beautifully and powerfully that he who builds for this world, builds for a glory that is temporary, but he who builds for the next world, builds for a glory that is everlasting.

Shehzade Mosque:

A Monument to Parental Sorrow – and Favouritism

Sultan Suleiman the Magnificent loved his eldest son, by Hurrem, very much. In fact, as soon as Mehmet was born, he started to show favouritism towards him, over his eldest son and crown prince Shehzade Mustafa.

Mehmet was a good prince although he was nowhere near as talented and loved by the people as Mustafa. For many years, tension was building where it was clear that only one of them would win the throne and the other, in accordance with the laws of the Ottoman family, would be executed.

The competition between the two ended abruptly when Shehzade Mehmet died of smallpox. Suleiman was heartbroken and ordered Sinan to build a magnificent mosque in honour of the young prince.

Some of Suleiman's children like Shehzade Mehmet, Sultan Selim II and Princess Mihrimah had beautiful mosques built in their memory. Others like Mustafa, Jahangir and Bayezid died violent deaths and were all but ignored by Suleiman at the end. The Shehzade mosque is an example of an early Sinan Mosque. This is where he experimented with new techniques and you can see he is trying to work out his signature style. However, it also symbolises something more deep on behalf of the one commissioning it – paternal sorrow and the dangers of favouritism.

Shehzade Mosque:
The other Shehzade with no Mosque

Shehzade Mustafa was the JFK of his people – a glamorous and charismatic leader tragically cut down before his potential could be fulfilled. But the story of Mustafa is beyond tragedy – a new word would need to be invented in the English language to adequately describe the fall of this shooting star, the greatest Sultan who never ruled.

He was the eldest son of Sultan Suleiman by the formidable and beautiful Mahidevran. But despite being born a prince into a life of luxury, he worked hard and became a warrior, a poet, an intellectual and a statesman. He was the human face of the Empire and became so loved by the common people that his prestige began to rival even that of the magnificent Sultan himself.

But powerful men have powerful enemies; and few were more powerful than his stepmother Hurrem. If Mustafa lived, her own sons would be executed due to the fratricidal laws of the Ottoman family. Like a mother cub protecting her own, she worked with the Grand Vizier Rustem Pasha (who also happened to be her son-in-law) to convince Suleiman that Mustafa was out to dethrone him. At first, Suleiman would not hear of it, but slowly the poisonous words had an effect. After all, had not Suleiman's own father overthrown his grandfather?

A trap was set by Rustem and Hurrem. Suleiman asked Mustafa to come to him whilst on expedition. Mustafa was warned again and again not to go and reassure his father from afar. He refused to accept this and insisted on going anyway. When he was informed in no uncertain terms by a friendly source in Suleiman's entourage, that he would be executed on arrival, Mustafa replied in words that are greater than any conquest on the battlefield: "He is my father. It was he who brought me into this world. If he wishes, then he can take me out of it." Mustafa entered unarmed into his father's tent and was immediately strangled by mute executioners as his father watched. They would not know it then, but the decline of the Ottoman empire began that fateful day in Ereğli.

Respect for parents is enshrined in Islam. We are reminded often of their status and our rights and responsibilities towards them. Mustafa demonstrated to us the importance of parents in Islam, in a way that few can ever equal. Meanwhile, Suleiman failed to demonstrate the responsibility of a parent to return this love back with mercy and compassion. We could all do with being more like Mustafa and less like Suleiman.

Yavus Selim Mosque:

Selim "The Grim"

Selim came to throne the same way he ruled – in a blaze of fury that saw him steamroll all those who stood in his way. The son of Bayezid II, he rebelled against his father when he was passed over succession. By the end of the struggle, his brothers and nephews were dead, and his father exiled. But Selim "The Grim" – as he was to be known – was only just getting started.

Through stern determination and non-stop conquests, Selim tripled the size of the Ottoman Empire in just over eight years. His most significant conquest was that of Mameluke Sultanate in 1516. This victory brought most of the modern Middle East under his control including the Holy cities of Makkah, Madinah and Jerusalem. To crown it all, the last Abbasid Caliph Al Mutawakkil III, gave the ancient title to Selim. Hence, Selim became the first Caliph from the House of Osman.

Selim was known for his serious nature. "May you be a vizier of Selim" was a popular Ottoman curse that seems to have originated because of his nasty habit of executing his ministers on a regular basis. Indeed, some stories state that as soon as someone was appointed to an important position in his government, they would prepare their will!

The grim nature made him perfectly suited to bring order to his Empire and to the surrounding states. In his short reign he had multiplied the size of the nation manifold. It was said that he spent more time in the saddle than outside it. Therefore, fittingly, he is said to have died due to sirpence – an infection caused by spending too much time riding horses. Whatever his cause of death, being stern and grim are never endearing qualities and were it not for his successors that did much to ameliorate his reputation, we may well remember Selim rather differently today.

Yavuz Sultan Selim Mosque:
A Son's Love for his Father

The Yavus Selim Mosque is a monument to love: specifically, the love of a son for his departed father. When Sultan Suleiman the Magnificent ascended the throne, he had this complex built in memory of his father Sultan Selim. It is a familiar sight on the Istanbul skyline due to its excellent location atop one of the main hills of Istanbul.

Yavus Selim (Selim the Grim) spent most of his life in battle and built little in the way of grand buildings or mosques. He was too busy building an Empire. When he died at a relatively young age, he had not left any monumental place of worship to continue his good deeds after he died. Luckily, his son, Suleiman ensured that this oversight was rectified.

The mosque was built by a predecessor of Sinan's and although magnificent to look at, it makes you appreciate the quality of the master's work even more when you see how far he transcended his contemporaries. In any other city or country, the Yavuz Sultan Selim Mosque would be the most magnificent structure. In Istanbul, it struggles to make it into the top five.

The view from the gardens of the mosque out on to the Golden Horn is enchanting, but what is most impressive is the lengths a son would go to for the sake of his father's afterlife. Truly, for all of Selim's faults, he was still blessed to have a son like Suleiman. It is easy to forget that we are one of the gates to increasing the good deeds of our parents even after they are gone. If we want to honour their memory, we should do more good in their name and for our own sake too.

Yavus Selim and Abdul Majeed Tombs:

So close, yet so far

The tomb adjacent to that of Sultan Yavus Selim is that of his descendant Sultan Abdul Majeed, the son of Mahmud II.

Abdul Majeed was himself a transformative Sultan with all future Sultans bar Abdul Aziz being his children. He continued the reforms that his father set in motion culminating in the Tanzimat and the Hatt-i-Gulhane, westernisation reforms that removed the religious principles that the Ottoman Empire was based on and replaced it with something similar to that of a modern European state. While seemingly a great modernising move in order to try and catch up, a copy is never the same as the original and the reforms led to increased nationalisation and instability.

He was a man of contrasts, being largely responsible for the way the old section of the Prophet's mosque in Madinah looks today and is commemorated with having one of the entrances named after him. However, he was also the Sultan during the Crimean War and celebrated the triumph against Russia (only possible due to significant British and French support) by attending a waltz at the British Embassy and scandalising Ottoman society by dancing with the wife of the British ambassador.

One of his lesser-known accomplishments was instituting one of the first vaccination drives in the Muslim world whilst using his own funds to promote it. He ruled during the 1800's and was paranoid of catching infections which is ironic because Abdul Majeed was known to be sickly. Unfortunately for him, his paranoia was justified, and he died of Tuberculosis before his 40th year.

So it is that this garden contains the unusual combination of the tombs of arguably the fiercest and the most timid of all Ottoman Sultans next to each other. Both died of infections – one spending his life ignoring them and the other desperately trying to avoid them. Truly, to Allah we belong and to Him we will return.

Fatih Mosque:

The Conqueror's Mosque

If Eyüp is the historical Islamic centre of Istanbul, then Fatih is its current beating heart. Originally built on the ruins of the Byzantine Church of the Holy Apostles, the Fatih mosque was the very first of the Ottoman Imperial mosques and set the pattern that everyone was to follow thereafter.

The Church of the Holy Apostles was built by Constantine – the founder of Constantinople, to house the remains of all the apostles of Christ. He was only able to find one – that of St Andrew, as well as that of two other saints. In time, he and other Byzantine Emperors would be buried here.

Given current prejudices, it would be easy to assume that the Muslim conquerors had erased this holy church and unceremoniously scattered the remains of the Byzantine Emperors. However, nothing could be further from the truth with the marauding Crusaders having done this centuries earlier. To this day, the bodies of Constantine and Justinian remain missing with only the sarcophagi remaining.

The mosque you see in front of you is a 1700s building as the original was completely destroyed by three major earthquakes, the last of which left hardly anything of the original building usable. It is a testament to the revered place of Sultan Mehmet Fatih, that in the heart of his descendants and people that every incarnation of the mosque was still named for him rather than the builder.

Many important events of Islamic significance have taken place at the mosque. Here was the last time a sheikh-ul-Islam read out the proclamation for Holy War, when the Ottomans joined WWI on the side of the Germans.

Mehmet Fatih:

From Mehmet to Fatih

The Prophet Mohammed ﷺ is reported to have remarked once, "Verily you shall conquer Constantinople. What a wonderful leader will her leader be, and what a wonderful army will that army be!" Not many people can lay claim to having a prophecy praising them. But then again, Mehmet ibn Murad was no ordinary person.

He first became Sultan at the age of twelve when his father abdicated to concentrate more on his afterlife. However, when faced with a Hungarian invasion he realised the limits of his ability (something few rulers ever do) and asked his father to return and take the crown. When Murad II refused having grown accustomed to a life of reflection and prayer, Mehmet wrote to him, "If you are the Sultan, come and lead your armies. If I am the Sultan, I hereby order you to come and lead my armies." Faced with such irrefutable logic, Murad returned and became Sultan once more. The invading Hungarians did not stand a chance.

Not long after his father died, Mehmed – now a bit older and a bit more confident – accomplished the victory that would not only change the course of history, but also his name. He learnt multiple languages including Greek so that he could understand his enemy better. He made treaties and alliances with all who could possibly come to the aid of the Byzantines. Through a complex network of spies, he mapped out the entire city of Constantinople down to the resources available and the morale of the inhabitants. He commissioned the world's largest cannon and assembled an army that believed in his dream as much as he did. After all this, he declared, "Either I will take Constantinople or Constantinople will take me."

After years of preparation, Mehmed removed the thorn in the side of almost every Muslim ruler until that point. He conquered Constantinople and he did it in epic style in a series of events that included rediscovering the tomb of Abu Ayyub Al Ansari (see Eyüp section) and sailing his navy over land.

More than any other person, Mehmed made his mark on this city. From the Topkapı palace to the Grand Bazaar, from the legacy of interethnic harmony to the rules of governing an Empire – he had a hand in them all. He died after being poisoned at the age of 49 on his way to yet another conquest. In a mark of the greatness of the man, Church bells rang across Christendom in celebration at the passing of this most dangerous foe. Meanwhile the Muslims lamented the passing of the one who would forever be simply known as "The Conqueror."

When you visit his tomb, pay special attention to the framed hadith hanging over the wall next to the headstone. There, you will see his greatest victory, hanging over his head – the hadith of the Prophet ﷺ about him.

Mehmet Fatih:

The ingredients of a legend

The more you read about the life of this man, the more you get a glimpse of his greatness. For instance, he was fluent in Greek, Latin, Arabic, Persian and Hebrew – in addition to his native Ottoman Turkish. He did this not just to while away the time at court, but so that he could get interpret intelligence from Constantinople first hand.

He set up his army to use psychological warfare with the playing of drums and noise that accompanied the irregular bashibazouks, but pindrop silence frightening the enemy when Janissaries rolled in.

He had surrounding potential enemies neutralised through marriage, alliances or paying them off. Thus he made sure that when Constantinople called for help, there would be no reply.

He encouraged healthy competition amongst his Viziers assigning each a tower to build on the Rumeli Hisari fortress and rewarding the first to complete their task.

In one memorable instance, he realised that his soldiers would respond more favourably to inspiration from one of their own, so he disguised himself as a soldier and gave a rousing speech to his "comrades." The disguise was only discovered afterwards.

It was said that he spent as much time poring over maps, old books of warfare and intelligence as he did in the field. He knew that victory would be earnt. He would do whatever was in his control, and leave to Allah whatever was not.

The Mosque of Sinan:

Substance over style

Sinan had spent his entire working life building projects at the behest of wealthy patrons. Whether it was a mosque, a tomb or a hammam, they told him their vision and he carried it out in the most beautiful way. There was one project that was different to all the others and it is only a short walk from Fatih mosque.

This mosque was built by Sinan for himself. There was no patron telling him what to do or what it should look like. There were no stylistic considerations or conventions that he needed to keep. He was able to let his creative instincts go completely free this time. He could do whatever he wanted to do.

As you get closer to this mosque, you notice that it is right in the heart of a busy neighbourhood. Finally, when it comes into view, you're left flabbergasted. It is extremely ordinary. There's almost no embellishment of any kind on the exterior or interior. If it were not for the extremely simple minaret, it would be easy to mistake it for a home or an office.

Even the minaret is ordinary. No overhanging balconies, no muqarnas, no calligraphy – in fact, nothing beyond a few windows from which to call out the prayer. On the inside, the building is just as spartan. Even that is putting it charitably.

Surely, there must be some mistake? Then it hits you. When given the opportunity to build something without any constraints, he chose substance over style. A mosque is a place of prayer, whether it be an architectural marvel that is visited by Millions across the world or a squat looking building nestled in a busy neighbourhood. The value of the mosque comes from those who use it and what they are using it for, not the architecture.

The master builder understood what so few others do. Beauty lies in the utility rather than in the aesthetics. Sinan was truly on a different level to the rest of us.

Molla Zeyrek Mosque:

Three Churches, One Mosque

In 1118, the Byzantine Empress decided to build a monastery on a hill overlooking the Golden Horn. The Christ Pantokrator (Omnipotent) had a library and hospital attached. However, Irene did not begin her life as an Eastern Orthodox Christian. She was the orphaned Catholic daughter of a former ruler of Hungary and sufficiently distant enough to be used to forge an alliance with the Byzantines. She devoted her life to the welfare of her people and upon her death, she was declared a saint.

Her husband, the Emperor John Komnenos built another church adjacent to Christ Pantokrator dedicated to her and Mary. Eventually, the two twin churches were connected by a third church dedicated to St Michael. This middle connecting church would become the Imperial Mausoleum of the Komnenos and Palailogus dynasties.

It was used as a palace by at least one Latin Emperor who ruled after the Fourth Crusade sacked the city. However, after the restoration of the Byzantine Empire, it was once again converted to a monastery with the most famous occupant being Gennadius – the first head of the Eastern Orthodox to rule after the Muslim conquest.

After the conquest, the Churches were combined into one Mosque and named after the Molla Zeyrek. The Islamic preacher was one the most popular in Istanbul and a favourite of Sultan Muhammad Fatih himself.

The building remains a magnificent example of Byzantine architecture from the middle period. From the outside, it would be difficult to tell that it is now a Mosque, but even the interior gives you clues as to its past life. One may think that this is all that is left, but if you pull back the carpets at the edges, you will be surprised to see that it now lays on a raised false floor. The glass covering allows you to admire the magnificent Byzantine Opus Sectile floor tiles, intact and preserved.

The vagaries of history mean that the burial chambers of Byzantine Emperors who were implacable foes of the Muslim world are now part of a Mosque. It is the often-downplayed tolerance of Islamic civilization that means that the Ottoman rulers did not erase all traces of their vanquished foes and instead went through considerable trouble to preserve their works and their legacies.

The Mosque of the Rose:

A Final Prayer and Lasting Mystery

The Byzantine Emperor kneels at the altar along with his most loyal followers and soldiers. His Empire, in fact, the Roman Empire that has survived from the days of Augustus, is witnessing its last dawn.

The Ottomans have breached the impregnable walls of Constantinople and now there is nothing for it but to pray and fight. The church he chose to kneel in before he made his last stand was the rather anonymous Church of Saint Theodosia rather than one of the other major churches of the city.

During one of the iconoclastic periods that the Byzantines went through, the Emperor had ordered the destruction of a large image of Christ that stood over the main gateway to the Palace. As a soldier was removing it, Theodosia kicked away the ladder causing the soldier to fall and die. She was executed and reportedly her body was brought here. When the iconoclastic period was over and icons were all the rage in Byzantium again, she was celebrated as a martyr and eventually a saint. She became the patron saint of the sick and the disabled of Constantinople.

When the Ottomans conquered the city, they found the church garlanded with roses and hence the name Gul Mosque came about. The Church was converted into a Mosque and used mainly by those working in the naval dockyards. It remains a beautiful example of syncretism between Islamic and Orthodox styles.

The southeast part of the church has tombs which have conflicting stories. One of the stories is that it is the tomb of the famous Ottoman dervish Gul Baba. He was a contemporary of Sultan Suleiman and fought in his army during the conquest of Hungary. However, it is almost certain that he died in Budapest.

Another theory is that this is the resting place of the last Byzantine Emperor, although there is little evidence of this either.

St Mary of the Mongols:

Conquering the Khans

History is often written through sweeping events, large scale wars and great figures striding across the world stage. Sometimes, though, it turns on events so small that it is uncomfortable to acknowledge how pivotal they were. One of these "small" events was the marriage of the Byzantine Princess Maria Palailogina.

Princess Maria was sent to marry Hulagu Khan, the grandson of Genghis Khan and now ruler of the ilkhanate. Hulagu has just done what the Byzantines could never do, destroyed the Abbasid Caliphate and ravaged the Muslim lands from Samarqand to Damascus. Clearly, the Mongols were in ascendancy and before they could adopt the religion of Islam, the Byzantine Emperor was going to try to win over these new conquerors to the fold of Christianity.

Maria was his secret weapon. Beautiful, a princess (even though illegitimate) and deeply religious, she would be less a loving wife and more a zealous missionary. However, on her way to marry Hulagu, news reached of his death. As this union had nothing to do with love, the party pressed forward with hardly a pause with the new intended bridegroom being the son of Hulagu, Abaqa Khan.

Maria became incredibly influential in Mongol court and spread the influence of Christianity. She sought and gained special protection for Christians in the Empire and for 15 years was well on her way to possibly making the Mongol Empire into a Christian one. However, in yet another twist of fate, Abaqa died and was succeeded by his brother Ahmed – who was a devout Muslim.

Within a short space of time, he embedded Islam into the royal court so much so that future Khans had to outwardly profess Islam even if they were not so sure about their religious convictions in private. Maria found herself persona non grata and made her way back to Constantinople.

She was sent out once more to negotiate with the Ottomans, but her clear hatred of Muslims served to only inspire the Ottomans to greater victories. She retired to this monastery which still bears her name. Had her marriage lasted longer and had her influence extended to eliminating

Ahmed from court, the Mongols may well have become a Christian dynasty ruling Muslim lands and we may never have seen the rise of the Moghuls of India, the Timurids of Central Asia or the Golden Horde in the Caucuses.

This monastery is also known to the Ottomans as the "Church of Blood" as it was the scene of violent hand to hand combat during the Conquest of 1453. The road leading up to the Church is still called "Ascent of the Standard Bearer" after this key member of the Ottoman army gained martyrdom here.

Pertevniyal Mosque:

Mother Knows Best

This mosque is well worth a visit; full of character and a homely charm that is perfectly in keeping with its patron. Pertevniyal was the feisty Eastern European wife of Sultan Mahmud II.

She was a live wire who was as much a stickler for tradition as her husband was not. There are many people who accuse her of being a meddling know-it-all. However, I would put forward a different view. She was the one who kept the royal family grounded to the needs of the common person. She was always mistrustful of Midhat pasha, the Vizier who others say was the mercurial wunderkind, but in reality, killed one Sultan, overthrew another and destabilised the third.

She was also the Valide Sultan who put some checks on her own son, the rotund yet likeable Abdul Aziz. She asked him to cut short his long trip to Europe, so the Empire was not without a leader at that time. She told him off when he walked through Beylerbeyi Palace arm in arm with the Empress of France. She also threw a statue he had made of himself in the sea as she (like most pious Muslims) saw it as an abomination.

The young prince Abdul Hamid II would spend much of his time in the Harem with her. Having lost his mother at a very young age and not found much love from his father, Sultan Abdul Majid I, the shy young prince would spend most of his time with the fascinating old woman who was the favourite wife of his grandfather. In return, she told him plenty of stories, imbibed in him a love of Islam and piety and taught him how to navigate successfully through the world of the Harem.

When Sultan Abdul Aziz committed suicide (or was assassinated, as was most likely), she was pitied, but within months, she had her revenge. Her young protégé, now Sultan Abdul Hamid II, executed Midhat Pasha for regicide and treachery.

Hırka-I Şerif Mosque:

A Ramadan Gift

In the Hırka-i Şerif neighbourhood lies this mosque that is off al-most all itineraries, but really should not be. The mosque houses the Hırka-i-serif – the mantle of the Prophet (SAW.) This is said to be the mantle that the Prophet ﷺ gifted to Uwais Al-Qarni. It is only displayed in Ramadan though so you would have to time your visit accordingly.

Uwais al-Qarni was an almost sahaaba. A sahaaba (literally, Companion) is considered anyone who saw the Prophet ﷺ while alive and died as a Muslim. Uwais was a contemporary of the Prophet ﷺ and longed to see him, but was also the sole carer of his elderly mother so could not leave her. Knowing his predicament, the Prophet ﷺ advised him to serve his mother and compensated him by sending him his own mantle.

Eventually, when his mother passed away, Uwais hurried to Madinah to see the Prophet ﷺ but unfortunately arrived to find that he too had recently passed. He then became foremost amongst the second generation known as the tabi'un.

The mantle, like most Ottoman artefacts, has good provenance. It was passed to the descendants of Uwais Al-Qarni, but Umayyad rulers induced them to "sell" it to them. It then remained in the Caliphal treasury until it passed from them to the Abbasids and, eventually, from the Abbasids to the Ottomans at the conquest of Egypt. This mantle has been preserved and guarded by Empires and emperors so that today we can enjoy this treasure and legacy from the Prophet ﷺ himself.

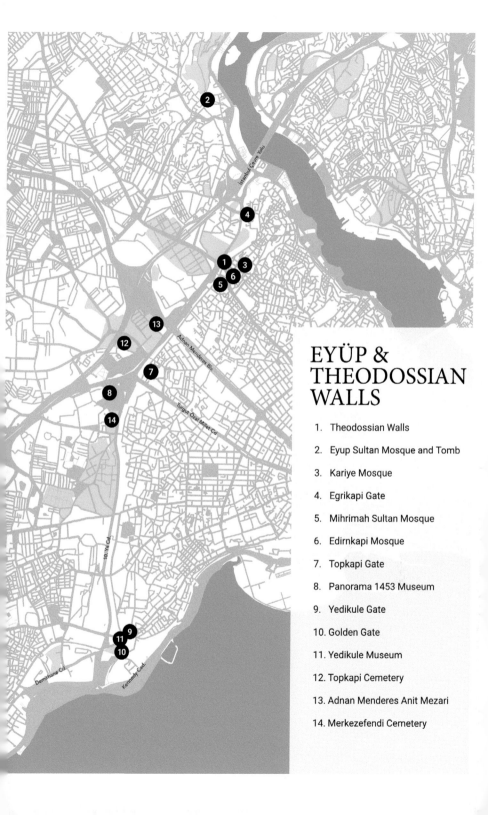

EYÜP & THEODOSSIAN WALLS

1. Theodossian Walls

2. Eyup Sultan Mosque and Tomb

3. Kariye Mosque

4. Egrikapi Gate

5. Mihrimah Sultan Mosque

6. Edirnkapi Mosque

7. Topkapi Gate

8. Panorama 1453 Museum

9. Yedikule Gate

10. Golden Gate

11. Yedikule Museum

12. Topkapi Cemetery

13. Adnan Menderes Anit Mezari

14. Merkezefendi Cemetery

Eyüp Sultan Tomb:

The Seed of Madinah

Most people in their 80's have retired, slow down and want to spend the remaining time they have on Earth surrounded by their family. This was not the case for Abu Ayyub al-Ansari (R.)

Abu Ayyub (R) was a very special companion of the Prophet (SAW.) When the Prophet ﷺ first arrived in Madinah, everyone wanted the honour of hosting him. The Prophet ﷺ did not want to hurt the feelings of anyone or any tribe. The Prophet ﷺ advised the jostling crowd that his camel Qaswa was under divine direction. Wherever the camel stopped, there the Prophet ﷺ would stay.

Surely enough, eventually Qaswa stopped in the location which was where the Prophet's Mosque now stands. Adjacent to this plot of land was the home of Abu Ayyub (R) who, in an act of decisive quick action, he quickly picked up the baggage of the Prophet ﷺ and took it into his home.

Abu Ayyub (R) thus became the neighbour and host of the Prophet ﷺ and eventually his standard bearer. Many years after the Prophet ﷺ had passed away, this famous Sahaaba decided instead to join the first Muslim expedition against Constantinople.

The expedition was not well thought out and the legendary walls of the city as well as the harshness of the winters meant that the Muslims were unlikely to succeed and Abu Ayyub (R) himself was dying and requested that his body be placed on a plank, that the Muslims charge as far as they could go and bury him there. Perhaps, one day, others will find him, he reasoned.

This they did and the grave of Abu Ayyub disappeared from sight of Muslims till rediscovered by Mehmet Fatih and his teacher Akshamsuddin centuries later. There are some stories that the grave was known to the Byzantines and even revered as that of a holy saint, although there is difference of opinion as to the authenticity of this. Ever since then, this has been the holiest location in Istanbul and every Sultan upon ascension has come here to be girded with the sword of Osman Ghazi at the grave of this mighty Sahaaba.

Truly the companions of the Prophet ﷺ were not buried, they were seeds of faith planted in the ground and generations after generations of Muslims are the fruit from those blessed seeds.

Eyüp Minaret:

The Ramadan Mahya

If you visit during Ramadan, you will be able to witness a centuries' old tradition that is unique to Türkiye. The Mahya were candles that were placed on strings that ran between two minarets. The candles would spell out Islamic phrases or verses from the Quran and the occasional image.

Even though the effect is mesmerising today, it simply cannot compare to the sheer visual impact the Mahya would have in a time before the current level of light pollution. In a pre-industrial era, the night sky being emblazoned with words that are seemingly floating in mid-air must have made quite the visual impact.

Eyüp Sultan Mosque:
The Pride of the Nation

It can be no secret that for many decades, the Turkish nation has had a complicated relationship with Islam. In one fell swoop, it had gone from the seat of the Muslim world to a secular nation where no faith ruled, and Islam in particular was suppressed.

Things had been changing though. Decades of perseverance and a steady process of evolution rather than the short-cut instability of revolution was being used to reacquaint Turks with their faith and their heritage.

I was aware of this as I saw more and more Turkish women adopting the hijab and even making it fashionable. There were also young Turkish men with beards and the mosques did not seem as abandoned as I was led to believe by previous visitors.

But what really made me realise that things were changing was a little sign near the grave of Abu Ayyub Al-Ansari (R). On it was written a simple note. "This is the grave of Eyüp Ansari. This is the grave of the standard bearer of the Prophet ﷺ. This is the pride of our nation."

Mihrimah Sultan Mosque:

A Rare Honour

Mihrimah was the favourite daughter of Sultan Suleiman the Magnificent. She had Sinan build this majestic and almost feminine looking mosque for her. In fact, it was the second mosque he built for her – the first being built almost two decades earlier in the Üsküdar district across the Bosphorus and well worth a visit.

Mihrimah is Persian for "sun and the moon" and legend states that if you can be in position to see both mosques at the same time from a vantage point on the anniversary of her birth, you will see the sun set behind the minaret of the Edirnekapı mosque and the moon rise between the minarets of the Üsküdar mosque.

There are stories that this rare honour of two mosques by Sinan for the same person is because he was in love with her, but there is no evidence of this. What there is evidence of is the beautiful, graceful architecture of both mosques that stand in silent tribute to their patron.

The life of an Ottoman princess was full of luxury and wealth, but tragedy played a part too. Ottoman princesses could not choose who they married and were often paired off with much older distinguished statesmen. The statesmen themselves equally had little say in the matter and were forced to divorce their current wives.

Therefore, it is unsurprising that Ottoman princesses often concentrated their efforts on charitable causes. Mihrimah was no exception and had not one, but two mosques built by Sinan on the Asian and European sides of the city.

We are not always in control of what happens to us, but we are in control of how we handle what life throws at us. Ottoman princesses dealt with the terrible way their lives were controlled by channelling their energies into helping those less fortunate than themselves. You are never plunged into so much darkness that you cannot shine a light for someone else.

Kariye Mosque:

Iconoclasm and Tawhid

This building was originally a church and monastery, then turned into a mosque and then into a museum. Although not much of the original building survives, the preponderance of Byzantines mosaics are a treasure trove for those interested in pre-Islamic Constantinople.

While the reversion of the Kariye Mosque back to the Chora Church was very controversial for pious Muslims everywhere, this is far from the only controversy attached to the building. The many icons contained within it were at one time the source of intense debate in the Eastern Orthodox church itself.

Swayed by the Islamic prohibition of making images of living creatures as sacrilegious, a movement sprung up in Eastern orthodoxy that vociferously argued the same. They were called "iconoclasts" – literally the destroyer of images used in religious worship.

There were at least two well-known iconoclastic periods during the Byzantine Empire where all images were destroyed and seen as heretical. They lasted for several decades each, but their effect was more deleterious on Byzantine art than the ensuring four centuries of Muslim rule. So many Byzantine works of art were destroyed in those periods that it makes those that survived in churches like the Chora even more valuable.

It is interesting to note how a united and powerful Muslim world was deemed worthy of emulation, not just in culture and science but in matters of faith as well. Today, the Church turned Museum is once again being made into a Mosque.

Panorama 1453 Museum:

History Brought to Life

Many Muslim nations can be accused of being ignorant of their own history. However, Türkiye was not so much ignorant of its history as it was disgusted by it. For decades the official government line was that everything Ottoman was backward, barbaric and not worthy of remembering.

This panoramic museum is an attempt to redress the imbalance caused by such a myopic historical view. It chronicles arguably the greatest moment in Ottoman history, where the city of Constantinople was finally conquered by Sultan Mehmet Fatih.

Part of the museum is your standard museum set-up with posters, pictures and exhibits about the life of Mehmet Fatih and the conquest of the city. The other part is an immersive panoramic exhibition with a well-known painting of the time being enlarged to cover a huge planetarium like structure. Together with sound effects, props and audio-visual tricks, it gives the viewer as close an impression as possible to being in the thick of battle.

It is important for history to come to life in a way that can inspire others to not only be proud of their past, but to forge a better future. This interactive museum does this in spades and helps rehabilitate a part of Turkish history that has been neglected for far too long.

Abu Shayba Al Khudri:

The Tomb of the Lesser Known Sahaaba

While there are a multitude of sources indicating that Ayyub Al-Ansari (R) was buried outside the then known walls of Constantinople in the first century of the Hijrah, there is much less information about any other Sahaaba who may be similarly resting beneath the ground in Istanbul.

Out of the other graves that are claimed to belong to that of companions of the Prophet ﷺ, the one that has the most claim to legitimacy is that of Abu Shayba Al Khudri (R). The grave is located in the Eyüp district at the foot of the massive Byzantine walls.

Ibn ʿAbd al-Barr in his book *al-Istīʿāb* narrates a hadith that is said to have been transmitted via this Sahabi who died in the "Land of Rum." This is not enough to indicate that he was buried near the walls of Constantinople, much less the location of the tomb being accurate. It is good to maintain a healthy scepticism about the veracity of it and the other purported graves of Sahaaba in Istanbul.

The first proper Muslim assault on the city took place up many decades after the death of the Prophet ﷺ during the reign of Muawiya (R), by which time most Sahaaba would have passed or were extremely elderly and therefore less likely to have been part of the army. Those tombs that are located within the old walls of the city will have a hard time explaining how they ended up there when Muslims did not breach the walls for centuries after the hijrah. Those outside the wall may have more of a claim to legitimacy, but again, more research is needed.

Yedikule:

The Prison with a Golden Gate

If Constantinople was to have a main entrance, then it would have to be as grand as the city itself. The Golden Gate (Porta Aurea) does not disappoint. A triumphal archway flanked by tall towers, monumental statues of Emperors and relief works depicting the life of Hercules, the Golden Gates were a ceremonial entrance reserved for the most important occasions.

One such occasion occurred during the lifetime of the Prophet Muhammad ﷺ, when the Emperor Heraclius entered the gates in triumphal procession after defeating the Persians in one of the greatest comeback stories of the ancient world. This fulfilled a prediction found in the Quran, one which the Quraish openly mocked as ludicrous at the time of its revelation.

"Rome has been defeated in a nearby land. Yet following their defeat they will triumph." [Quran 30: 2 -3]

After the Ottoman conquest, the indefatigable Muhammad Fatih built a few extra towers and enclosed the area into a fortress complete with seven towers. Each tower contained different treasures, one for gold, one for silver ingots, precious jewels, documents etc. However, the treasury was moved into Topkapı palace, where it remains to this day and so the tower was used to store a different type of precious item – VIP prisoners.

Everyone from ambassadors to Kings, Emperors to Sultans of the Crimean Khanate, have been "guests" of the Sultan in Yedikule. In a cruel twist of irony, by far, the most important prisoner of Yedikule was Sultan Osman II, the young son of Sultan Ahmed, who made the fatal mistake of crossing the Janissaries. Rather than face his wrath, they imprisoned and executed him here.

Hucum Kapi:

The Gate of the Assault

The Ottoman soldiers had just completed yet another unsuccessful foray to the walls of Constantinople. The walls still looked unbreachable, and the defenders still held on tenaciously. They had thrown everything they had at the city. They had built and used the world's largest cannon, they had dragged their fleet overland and into the golden horn, they had sacrificed thousands of lives and yet the walls still held. If they were going to take the city, they would need a miracle.

And then, suddenly, they had one. One of the soldiers noticed something out of the corner of his eye. It was after dusk and the landscape was getting darker by the minute, but he thought he saw a sliver of light coming from the wall itself.

He looked closer and his heart started to pound within his chest. It was indeed a sliver of light. He had just discovered a secret door in the walls. It seemed that one the Byzantine defenders had been sloppy at closing it properly when they had slipped back into the city. Quickly he shouted to his comrades and turned around. They poured in through the secret gate. Seeing what was happening, the rest of the army followed close behind.

This gate became known as Hucum Kapi or Gate of the Assault. Constantinople had fallen.

Many Empires had attempted to protect themselves from downfall by building huge protective walls to keep the invading hordes out. Few were as successful as the Byzantines. The walls of Constantinople were one of the military wonders of the world. Their design, width and composition made them impenetrable for century after century.

Rome had fallen to the barbarians and the Goths, but Byzantium would continue to stand for centuries yet. Perhaps, it would have continued to survive for centuries more, and the last Roman Emperor would not have died desperately trying to close the breach, had the last man in had closed this gate properly.

The Gates of Constantinople:

The Stories Behind each Wall

The different gates of this wall are each a location of some significant event or personality. Despite their dilapidated state currently, it is easy to get a sense of the awe they would have inspired.

If you start at the northernmost end of the wall, there is a Byzantine palace called the Tekfur Palace. This was part of a larger palace on the site and was used by the Byzantine royalty during sieges to allow for proximity to the defenders. It was later converted into a menagerie and then a brothel, before being made into the museum it is now.

Topkapı gate is where the largest cannon in the arsenal of Muhammad Fatih was placed opposite, pounding the walls day and night. You can still find some of the gigantic cannonballs littered around this door, presumably so heavy that no one in 500 years has been able to lift them. Muhammad Fatih pitched his tent nearby.

Mesoteichion gate was where the very first Ottoman breach was made by Ulubatli Hassan. Despite being showered by arrows and having to scale a wall several stories high, he managed this superhuman feat and planted the Ottoman flag at the top of the tower. The sight emboldened the Ottoman army and disheartened the Byzantine defenders. Ulubatli Hassan collapsed under the weight of 27 arrows, but it was too late. He had written his name in the pages of history.

The Edirnekapı Gate was the gate through which Muhammad Fatih entered the city, a scene immortalised in paintings and frescos through the ages. This gate now has a large Turkish flag hanging on it. Just beyond the gate is one of the largest cemeteries of Istanbul, the Edirnekapı Cemetery which was the final resting place of many of the Ottoman soldiers who fell taking the city.

Adnan Menderes Anit Mezari:

An Unlikely Martyr

Adnan Menderes had a tragic childhood. Before his 10th birthday, he had lost his father, mother and sister. His father had been a wealthy landowner and thus the lonely young, orphaned boy was at least financially well off. He eventually grew up to be a successful lawyer and cotton farmer in Aydin.

After distinguishing himself in the Turco-Greek War, he eventually joined the CHP, the main party founded by Mustafa Kemal. However, he found himself in trouble due to his outspoken views and desire for a more democratic system. Along with a few like-minded friends, he set up the Democratic party. There was no hope of this party as the elections were not free or fair. Their only hope for success was a complete change of the geopolitical situation.

That change came at the end of World War II. Türkiye found itself surrounded by a lot of nations angry with it for having stayed neutral till literally the last few months of the war. Now, in order to survive the threat from Communist Russia, they had to truly embrace democracy or risk going behind the rapidly falling iron curtain. The first free and fair elections in the history of Türkiye brought Adnan Menderes to power in a landslide.

For the next decade he dominated Turkish politics with his boundless energy. He invested in the old capital, Istanbul, often waking up in the middle of the night with yet another idea on how to improve the lives of the ordinary people. He was obsessed with helping the poor and the common person, often at the expense of the elite.

Naturally, the army, the intellectual classes and the old guard hated him. but their hatred turned to sheer rage when he started giving concessions to the place of Islam in public life. Adnan was not a traditionally devout Muslim. He drank alcohol, had affairs and smoked cigars, but he did believe in Islam, and he put his energy into reversing the extremes of Kemalism.

The adhaan could be given in Arabic once more (the ban memorably lifted on the first day of Ramadan), mosques were refurbished and even Imam Hatip schools were reopened. He had his faults too. He became increasingly autocratic and embittered by the constant attacks. This was too much for the secular elite and eventually a coup was launched against him and his entire government. After a sham trial, he and his finance and foreign ministers were sentenced to death by hanging. On the morning of 17th September 1961 – Adnan Menderes, the legitimate Prime Minister of Türkiye put down his Quran and marched to the gallows to become a martyr.

Thirty years later, his body and that of his two friends, were moved from the island of Imrali to the current tomb so that they could forever be remembered for the ultimate sacrifice they paid. A sacrifice that meant that Islam may survive in Türkiye to this today.

BEŞIKTAŞ & BOSPHORUS

1. Istiklal Avenue

2. Taksim Square

3. Kabatas terminus

4. Bezmi Alem Valide Sultan Mosque

5. Dolmabahce Palace

6. Naval Museum

7. Hayreddin Barabarossa Tomb

8. Ciragan Palace

9. Ortakoy Mosque

10. 15th July Martyrs Bridge

11. Yildiz Palace

12. Malta Pavilion

13. Yildiz Hamidiye Mosque

14. Harbiye Military Museum

Dolmabahçe:

General

The Dolmabahçe palace was the home of the latter Ottoman Sultans –
and probably the most obvious symbol of their decline. Built on the orders
of the modernising Sultan Abdul Mejid I, Dolmabahçe was designed to be
the opposite of Topkapı in every way possible.

Whereas Topkapı was a series of organically added pavilions,
Dolmabahçe was a single perfectly proportioned building. Whereas
Topkapı was all about history and wielding power from the centre of
Government, Dolmabahçe was about luxury and seclusion.

Topkapı was the last in a long line of Muslim palaces before modern
times, from the Lal Qila in Delhi to the Alhambra in Granada. Dolmabahçe
was more in keeping with Buckingham Palace and the Élysée.

Although huge sums were spent on Dolmabahçe, it somehow still
fails to be anywhere near as impressive as Topkapı. Where pillars of solid
marble were once used, now plaster covered pillars with paint made to
imitate marble stand. Instead of craftsmanship perfected over centuries
and produced solely for the palace, items were brought in from Paris and
London. Instead of sumptuous Iznik tiles, there were painted wooden
walls.

The drop in architectural standards is far from the saddest part of
the story of Dolmabahçe. Some of the greatest tragedies of the Ottoman
Empire, and of Islamic history, took place within its walls as you shall find
out.

Dolmabahçe:

Caught Between Two Worlds

Sultan Abdul Majeed I was the son of his father – that is, he continued the modernising trend of his father Sultan Mahmud II. Under his reign, the Ottoman Empire tried to become a modern nation state. I emphasise the word "tried" because the Ottoman Empire was always caught between its Islamic past and the European future that Sultan Abdul Majeed and the latter Sultans seemed to relentlessly pursue.

Sultan Abdul Majeed personified this split-personality attribute that still affects the Muslim world today. He took his role as Servant of the Holy Cities seriously and ordered the full-scale renovation of many Islamic sites including Masjid Nabawi (the look of the old Mosque and the Green colour of the dome are his legacy.)

However, he also turned up to the British consulate to celebrate victory over Russia in the Crimean War and danced a waltz with the wife of the Ambassador. This scandalized Ottoman society as it was considered vulgar and un-Islamic by the majority of his subjects.

This shift from old to new was most evident when he decided to shift out of his ancestral home of Topkapı Palace and into the brand new, but gaudy Dolmabahçe Palace. Much like the Sultan itself, the new palace was pseudo-European, over the top and somehow, despite all the trappings of wealth, entirely lacking in self-confidence.

Dolmabahçe:

Sultan Mehmed Vahideddin

As you enter Topkapı, you cannot help but notice the picturesque area that leads onto the Bosphorus. The stunning sapphire waters of the Bosphorus contrast sharply with the white marble of the palace, with monumental gates and moorings adding to the opulence.

Sultan Mehmed ascended to the throne during the middle of the disastrous WWI for the Ottomans. Within months of the conclusion of the War, the Empire had lost much of its territory including Palestine to the British, Syria to the French and the Hijaz to the British and their proxies, the Sharifs.

To top it all off, the victorious allied powers had occupied Istanbul itself as part of the unjust treaties that followed the Ottomans to surrender. But despite all the crushing defeats and humiliations, what hurt most of all was the feeling that the Sultan was collaborating with the occupiers. This fuelled an anti-monarchy sentiment in the populace that built up like a powder keg waiting to explode. All that was needed was someone to light the match.

Enter Mustafa Kemal, the leader of the Grand National Assembly. By virtue of being the only man to stand up to the occupying forces, he gained the respect of his colleagues and countrymen. He used his popularity to skilfully push back against the occupiers and eventually exploit the resentment of the people to abolish the monarchy. The Ottoman Empire had come to an end.

Just as glorious as the entrance of the first Sultan Mehmed was into Constantinople, the exit of the last Sultan Mehmed was correspondingly pathetic. He sent a telegram to the British saying he feared his life was in danger and asked for protection from his own people. The last Sultan went into exile on board the British warship Malaya, stepping off the Quay at Dolmabahçe and closing a chapter of history.

He wished to retire to Makkah or Madinah but the British feared that the people may rally around him again. Instead, he was sent to San Remo, Italy where his old childhood friend, the King of Italy, offered him a palace. Sultan Mehmed refused as he felt it undignified for a former

Caliph to live on handouts. He eventually died penniless, living in a shack with his wife and son. His body was smuggled out in a carpet through the back door while creditors waited at the front. He is buried in a modest grave in Damascus at the Süleymaniye Mosque built by his much more magnificent ancestor.

Ceremonial hall:

To Inspire Awe

Every palace needs a room that will leave visitors in no doubt about the power and prestige of the owner. For Versailles, it is the Hall of Mirrors. For the Forbidden City it is the Hall of Supreme Harmony. For Dolmabahçe, this was achieved by the Ceremonial Hall known as the Muayede Salonu. Located next to the Mabeyn (literally, the in-between area) where the Sultan did most of his official work, the grand Ceremonial Hall was the apex of the palace experience.

It is not just European influenced, but European furnished and designed. The chandelier is from London, the dome itself would seem more at home in Rome than in Istanbul and the design is thoroughly French. Even the most unobservant of visitors could not help but realise that this was an Empire that was no longer proud of its own history, culture or art and instead slavishly imitated that of others. This was also the location of many an important event in the final dying days of the Ottoman Empire and afterward.

Sultan Murad V, the older half-brother of Sultan Abdul Hamid II, was enthroned here rather than at Topkapı in a break with tradition. Although, when they had deposed him a few weeks later, they probably wished they had stuck to the old ways.

Sultan Abdul Hamid II abandoned the palace within a year and only returned to celebrate major events like Eid festivals here. When he did, he would be sat on the throne and the room would be filled with the great and the good of the Empire each approaching the throne and kissing the hem of the cloth that draped it.

It was the location where Mustafa Kemal set forth his vision to change the Turkish alphabet from the Arabic script to the Latin one. In one stroke, he had successfully severed the connection of his people with their history and many aspects of their faith.

Eventually, when he died of alcoholic liver cirrhosis, his body was laid in state here for a grateful populace to file past. The Muayede Salon is very evocative without any of the trappings of luxury and power present today. It is still used as a favourite formal dinner venue for visiting foreign heads of states.

The Library of Abdul Majeed II:

The End of History

Imagine the pain, the suffering, the poignancy of the still smouldering ground zero on the morning of September 12th, 2001. It is a scene that cannot help but conjure up, not just the tragedy of what happened the day before, but the thousands of tragedies that this one brought into existence.

This small room is the ground zero of Islamic history. Save the piece of land that our Prophet ﷺ passed away on and his grandson was beheaded on, arguably no other place has witnessed a scene as devastating to the Muslim world as this.

And yet, on the face of it, this is just a library. It used to be an antechamber used by the Sultan, but the last Caliph had it converted into a library for his personal use. In it you will find his wallet, a self-portrait of his over the doorway and leather-bound books on a variety of subjects.

March of 1924, a Quran sits on the table directly in front of you being read by Abdul Majeed II in the waning hours of the night. His reading is interrupted by a messenger from the Grand National Assembly. The Caliphate is abolished and the royal family has to leave the nation before Fajr or face execution. A fatwa had been signed by the last Sheikh-ul-Islam under duress, who had promptly fled with his family.

Initially he said that he would rather die than accept this decision, but the palace officials, women and children begged him to surrender otherwise they would all die. The telegram lines had been cut; the palace was surrounded. He sighed and left the palace with a few clothes and nothing else. The 101st and last Caliph went into exile and the Muslim world would never be the same again.

Abdul Majeed II ends up in Paris and dies in 1945. After Janaza at the Paris Grand Mosque, he remained unburied as it was felt that a Caliph should not be buried in non-Muslim lands. A decade later, his body was flown to Madinah to be buried in Jannat Al-Baqi. There, the first Caliph and the last Caliph are buried within a short distance of each other.

Dolmabahçe Palace:
Shrine to Ataturk

Perhaps there is no man who has loomed larger over Türkiye for the last 100 years than the one who passed away in this bed. At precisely 9:05am on the 10th of November 1938, Mustafa Kemal – or Ataturk as he would come to be known, died of liver cirrhosis. Years of alcoholism had finally caught up with him.

Who was Ataturk? Born into an inconsequential family in Greece, Mustafa Kemal rose the ranks of the military and quickly distinguished himself for his bravery and courage. Campaigns in Libya and the Balkans made him stand out as someone to watch, but it was the trench warfare at Galipolli where he became a household name.

The allies and Winston Churchill had hoped to invade Istanbul directly and knock the Ottoman Empire out of WWI. They thought it would be easy to do as the Turks were weak and backwards. However, a combination of German advisers and the heroism of many Ottoman soldiers meant that the allied forces never got further than Galipolli. Istanbul was safe and many were grateful to Mustafa Kemal for his heroism.

But Mustafa harboured a deep antipathy for the Ottoman family and had already taken a minor part in the coup against Sultan Abdul Hamid II. He was biding his time. When the Ottomans eventually surrendered and Istanbul was occupied by British and French troops, he found his moment. As the Ottoman Sultan Mehmed VI displayed his cowardice by not standing up against the occupation, Mustafa Kemal did. He began one of the first and most successful fight backs against colonialism and eventually succeeded in securing freedom for at least part of the Empire. For this, he became a hero to many across the world – and an inspiration for everyone from Muhammad Ali Jinnah to Reza Shah Pahlavi.

After he gained total power and had removed the occupying powers, Mustafa Kemal began to remake the new nation in a radically different image. He blamed all the woes of Türkiye on religion in general and the Ottomans in particular. He banned the adhan in Arabic. He closed most religious schools. He banned the Fez, turban and the hijab. He changed the Arabic script of Ottoman into a latinised version. He was even quoted as calling the Prophet ﷺ as "that immoral Arab."

He saw that Turkish society was widely accepting of his actions and eventually banned the Sultanate and then the office of the Caliphate. Türkiye would be an aggressively secular republic. Your views of Mustafa Kemal will largely be down to whether you feel Islam has any place in modern society or not. He is a polarising figure because he exposes the dichotomy within the Muslim world today. Even to this day, his death is marked every year at the same time showing that for many, he still inspires devotion.

Çırağan:
Bad habits Die Hard

We all know someone who is an all-round nice person, but has one serious bad habit that threatens to define them. The bad habit may be smoking, swearing or gambling. Well, Sultan Abdul Aziz was a nice guy, but he had some strange habits. For instance, there are stories of how he allegedly used to like chasing chickens around the throne room and eventually – after catching one – would lavish medals, sashes and honours on it. How one would pin a medal to a chicken has never been explained in the books that record these exploits. This might make him sound a bit mad, but it was not a particularly harmful vice. Besides the few traumatised chickens, no one was hurt.

However, his real bad habit was slightly more expensive and harder to ignore. He liked building palaces. "Liked" is a mild term for what was full of indulgence, to the extent that it ended up dethroning him.

Each palace he built at a dire financial time for his Empire served to increase the anger of his population. Eventually, matters came to a head and Abdul Aziz was forced to abdicate in favour of his alcoholic and mentally unstable nephew Murad V.

This palace eventually served as the prison for Murad V and his family when he also was dethroned shortly afterward. After Murad V died, it later became a Parliament building. It was then converted into a football stadium and eventually fell into ruins.

Finally, an international hotel chain purchased the site and made it back into a hotel that even Abdul Aziz would have been comfortable in. Today you can visit Çırağan palace and stay in it. Although, despite the expensive furnishings and exorbitant price tag, it still does not meet the grandeur of the Sultans.

Yildiz:

Introduction

Fear is a dangerous thing. When it takes a hold of someone, even familiar surroundings become full of enemies and shadows. There can be no greater example of the perilous situation that the Ottoman. Empire found itself in than the fact that the last great Sultan did not feel safe in his own home.

Was it fear of outside forces, with the beautiful Bosphorus location of Dolmabahçe now looking vulnerable to attack by sea? Was it fear of assassins in the labyrinth of harem rooms as his uncle found in Topkapı? Was it fear of seeming ostentatious as Beylerbey palace turned out to be?

Whatever the reason, Abdul Hamid II ordered the court to be moved to the secluded woodland area of Yildiz – far from real or imagined threats. Gone was the confidence of Topkapı, the opulence of Dolmabahçe. This was the palace that fear built.

For nearly 30 years, the Empire and the Muslim world, was held together from this Palace largely by the untiring efforts of one man. Unfortunately, Yildiz could never provide a stable enough vantage point from which to give confidence to the people. It was an effort doomed to failure, but a valiant one all the same.

The Sale Kiosk:

Swiss Chalet

When a nation is in ascendancy, others attempt to copy them. When it is in decline, it inevitably imitates others. Such was the case with the very odd-looking Swiss Chalet that seems to have been transposed into the very heart of the city of Istanbul. It not only looks out of place, but makes little sense. Swiss chalets do not often get associated with a sense of majesty, power or even just an official workspace. Yet here it is attempting to do just that.

In addition, the Sale Kiosk was also meant to be the guest house for imperial visitors. One wonders how unimpressed they would be by this hotchpotch of different influences and styles, French crystal, Italian wall art, British furniture and so on. Thankfully the interior of the Ceremonial room managed to deliver in spades a regal splendour that would be befitting any Buckingham or Versailles. Still, if Dolmabahçe was a sign of the decline of the Ottomans, Yildiz was evidence of their impending collapse.

Yildiz:

The Baker Street Connection

Sultan Abdul Hamid II was a workaholic. He needed to be since he could not trust even his own ministers to do their jobs properly and without extensive corruption.

While watching a circus show in the palace theatre where a performer swallowed swords, he is said to have remarked drily, "So what? My Minister for War swallows up whole ships."

But micromanaging can only get you so far. Aides would find the Sultan reading through the candidates for a minor Police position in Damascus well past midnight. He would scrutinise every paper and bit of information and would often, fall asleep in his chair rather than in bed.

For a man with the level of stress and problems that he was facing, it is hard not to feel sympathy for the Sultan with real and imagined enemies lurking in every shadow and in every communique.

It was not all work though. He enjoyed watching demonstrations of Turkish wrestling as well as playing with his grandchildren. He liked to really unwind by having a servant read to him the serialised exploits of Sherlock Holmes.

In fact, when Sir Arthur Conan Doyle – the author of the Sherlock Holmes books – visited Istanbul, Sultan Abdul Hamid II presented him with one of the highest medals of honour. He also presented Mrs Doyle with a medal as she had taken a keen interest in feeding stray dogs during her brief stay in the city.

Many speculate as to what this Eastern potentate saw in the exploits of the thoroughly English detective. Some theorised that he used Sherlock as an inspiration for setting up his own vast network of spies and informants. Others felt he enjoyed the thought of someone being surrounded by enemies and being able to outsmart them all. Perhaps he just enjoyed a good story like the rest of us. Whatever the reason was, Sherlock provided Abdul Hamid II with brief periods of respite, in an increasingly dark atmosphere.

Yildiz:

The Malta Kiosk

The Malta Kiosk was made from beautiful limestone from the island of Malta, so much a preoccupation for previous Ottoman Sultans during their heyday.

It was one of many such pavilions dotting the landscape at Yildiz. It came in handy when Sultan Murad V was put under house arrest by his brother Sultan Abdul Hamid II.

It was even more useful when Midhat Pasha, a reforming Vizier, was eventually tried for treachery and the assassination of Sultan Abdul Aziz. Midhat Pasha is an enigmatic figure. As Grand Vizier, he tried to reform the Empire and bring in a constitution. However, he also changed some practices that were intrinsic to their culture too. He became a hero to revolutionaries and a figure of hate to those who wanted to preserve the status quo.

Whatever his true intentions were, in the end, he ended up on the wrong side of the Government and was tried in the garden outside this kiosk and eventually found himself meeting his end in a prison cell under mysterious circumstances.

Yildiz Hamidiye Mosque:

To Kill a Sultan

Sultan Abdul Hamid II was a complex character. Despite his appearance, hunched as if weighed down by the weight of the world, and old before his time – he was someone who it was impossible to be neutral about. People were either fanatically devoted to him or rabidly against him.

He knew this and therefore could never shake the feeling that an assassin was never far away. Forget individuals with a grudge, there were many powerful Empires that would like to see the back of him knowing that the future of the entire edifice of the Ottoman Empire lay in his hands.

He withdrew to the relative safety of the Yildiz palace in the hills above Istanbul. He was out of range of warships, and he was just far enough away to escape should he see a mob coming. However, there was one occasion on which he would be left exposed every single week, and that was the Selamlik.

The Selamlik was the traditional procession that Muslim rulers had to make on Friday to attend the congregational prayers. While daily prayers may be prayed at home or in the office due to extenuating circumstances, the Friday prayers were, by definition, congregational. They would also take place at the same time every week. All in all, they were an assassin's dream.

Knowing this Sultan Abdul Hamid II had the Yildiz Hamidiye mosque built close to Yildiz palace so that the route he had to take was short and relatively well-guarded.

Sultan Abdul Hamid II was right to be worried though. Armenian terrorists planted a large bomb in a carriage just outside the mosque. It was due to go off as the Sultan passed, but this Friday the Sultan unusually stopped to have a quick word with the Imam thus delaying him by a few minutes. The bomb went off killing 26 others and wounding more than 50, but the Sultan was saved and now more paranoid than ever. Although perhaps it is not paranoia if they are really after you.

Naval Museum:

From Warships to Kayaks

As a nation that started life in the deserts of Arabia, Muslims have had a complicated relationship with the seas from the very start. The Ottoman Empire fared better than other Islamic nations when it came to navigating the waves. The Naval Museum stands testimony to them being – for a time – the premier naval power in the Mediterranean, and occasionally beyond.

This niche museum is well worth a visit to witness so many important artefacts from the history of the Ottoman Empire. Pride of place must go to the links in the Byzantine chain that protected Constantinople from all sea-borne invaders.

Whenever the Byzantines were at risk of being attacked through the Bosphorus straits, they would raise the chain forming a simple but impenetrable obstacle to even the largest galleons. The story of how Muhammad Fatih overcame them is one that you simply have to hear to believe.

Other exhibits of interest are the military ships, standards from famous battles, busts of famous Ottoman admirals and the ever-elegant Kayaks. The Ottoman Sultans and nobility found the easiest way to get to different points in their city was to cross the Bosphorus. In the age before mega-bridges, the easiest way to do this was by Caiques (Kayaks) and you can see Imperial versions at the museum too.

It is interesting to note that earlier Ottoman naval artefacts from the 16th century and beyond were from their war ships that spread fear amongst the capitals of Europe and went toe to toe against the Portuguese as far afield as Indonesia and East Africa. Latter exhibits are mainly a host of Imperial pleasure boats from the 19th century, that spread nothing but Imperial largesse. While Britannia ruled the waves, the Ottomans had gone from one of the most effective navies in the world to a glorified taxi service. The Empire could not hope to survive long.

Naval Museum:

Gifts that sunk an Empire

It is not often that you can take a seat on the exact object that destroyed an Empire. But outside the Naval Museum in Istanbul, you can do just that when you see the propeller stuck on the floor.

Leading up to the First World War, all the world powers were scheming to get the Ottoman Empire on their side. Sultan Abdul Hamid II did his best to not allow the Muslim world to be drawn in on one side or the other, much to their consternation.

However, when the Young Turks dethroned him and installed his puppet younger half-brother Mehmed Reshad, they were able to change their neutrality. The only problem was that they were not united amongst themselves as to which side to join.

Eventually the cunning Enver Pasha managed to get his pro-German sympathies to win the day. The Germans knew that the Ottoman Empire was furious that two battle cruisers that they had recently purchased from the British Empire had not been delivered. Due to the upcoming war, the British had stolen these battlecruisers while still in the Scottish shipyards. To add insult to injury, these were paid for by public subscription i.e. by the general public.

The Germans deviously exploited the indignant feelings of the Ottoman public and sent two battlecruisers to attack the Russians in the Black Sea and then sought refuge in Istanbul. They radioed the Ottoman War Department run by Enver Pasha. Without seeking counsel from his colleagues, the Pro-German Enver agreed to accept the poisoned 'gift' of the two Battleship cruisers. Their flags changed from German to Ottoman, and they also hastily changed their name. The SMS Goeben became the Ottoman battlecruiser Yavus.

When the Russians saw this, they were furious and within hours, the Ottomans were at war with the Russian, French, British, Bulgarian and Italian Empires. Their fate was sealed.

Naval Museum:

Hayreddin Barbarossa

Born as Khizr on a Greek island, Barbarossa came from a family deeply in love with the sea. All of his brothers were well known captains and Khizr followed in his older brother's footsteps.

His older two brothers, Oruc and Ilyas were returning from a trading expedition in North Africa when they were captured by the Knights of St John. Ilyas was killed and Oruc was imprisoned. When Khizr discovered where his older brother was being held, he helped him escape and together with their other brother Ishak – they decided that they would never again let Crusaders or any European power control the Mediterranean.

They built a fleet and within a short space of time dominated the seas. When Oruc and Ishak died heroically defending the Moroccan city of Tlemcen from the Spaniards, Khizr was promoted to Kapudan Pasha – Admiral of the entire Ottoman navy. His exploits are legendary, from defending France to defeating the Holy League – there was no stopping him. By the time he retired, Khizr – or Hayrettin Barbarossa as he was now known, was the undefeated and undisputed master of the seas.

His tomb stands close to the naval museum, but is only open at certain times. There is a large statue of him in the square opposite. Even until relatively recently, whenever a Turkish naval vessel went to war, it would first stop at his tomb and salute him with cannon fire.

To be remembered after you pass is a blessing, but to be respected like this almost 500 years later is a legacy that few can claim.

The Military Museum:

Forged with Blood and Steel

Most Imperial capital cities have a military museum, but it would make sense that in the capital of a nation that had almost a mythical status on the battlefield, this would take pride of place. Originally, the museum was in Hagia Irene, on the grounds of Topkapı Palace. However, that site was deemed too small and so the Museum moved to the building that housed the Ottoman Imperial Military Academy.

This was where the best and brightest of the Empire were trained, like an Ottoman Sandhurst or Westpoint. They even have a recreation of what a scene in a classroom would have looked like, complete with mannequins representing their most famous graduates, including Mustafa Kemal.

The museum is huge and yet still can hardly contain the extensive number of exhibits within. You will find everything from the sword of Salahuddin's father to the mortars used to defend Gallipoli. The standards used by the Ottomans at the battle of Kosova and the Turkish National army in Korea sit side-by-side with the famous sea chain that protected Byzantium and swords belonging to Suleiman the Magnificent.

In addition to all the above, the Museum has sections dedicated to previous Turkish dynasties and the influence they have had on the rest of the world. From the Uyghurs in East Turkestan to the Seljuks in Anatolia, the exhibits act as a crash course on an often-underrepresented part of Islamic History.

History, especially Islamic history, tends to be reduced to our military successes and failures. While we must work to see beyond the battlefield, it is hard to deny that these fiery clashes of blood and metal do tell their own story of what a nation was willing to fight and die for.

Istiklal Cadessi:

The end of the Great Game

Running through the heart of Beyoğlu is a very strange street. Here, in this ancient Muslim city is a distinctly modern European avenue that feels like it has been transported straight out of the 8th arrondissement in Paris. It is not just the presence of grand shops with neoclassical facades or the proliferation of churches and consulates that give this impression; it is the entire atmosphere.

The street in question is called İstiklal Caddesi, but in Ottoman times it was more commonly known as the Grand Rue De Pera. When the European aristocracy referred to Istanbul as the Paris of the East or waxed lyrical about the mystery of the orient, they were thinking about here rather than the squalid streets of the old city.

The centre of gravity had decisively shifted from the palaces of the Sultans to here: the consulates of the great powers and the offices of their bankers. The decades before and after the first World War were an age of frenetic global activity. The world was more interconnected than ever with an expanding rail network and the introduction of flights. Most of the globe was now under the control of a handful of European nations. These nations competed at every level in a titanic contest known as "The Great Game" by the British and "The Tournament of Shadows" by the Russians.

This was the era of the Orient Express, Art Deco, great statesmen and international espionage. The fate of nations, especially in the Muslim world, was being discreetly negotiated in the drawing rooms of opulent hotels located here. Along with the hard power of diplomacy, politics and the military came the soft power of playwrights, artists and thinkers. Ernest Hemingway, Mark Twain, Greta Garbo, Tolstoy... the list is long and impressive. This combination of the iron fist of hard power followed by the velvet glove of soft power would continue to be a winning formula for Western armies and values to this day.

Today it is mainly full of shops and posh hotels, but do not let that fool you. A century ago, it would be everyone from Mustafa Kemal to Agatha Christie that walked these streets in search of power, glory or inspiration.

It remains one of the ironies of history that during the final decades of the Ottoman Empire, they lost their independence due to – in large part – what was happening here on Independence Avenue.

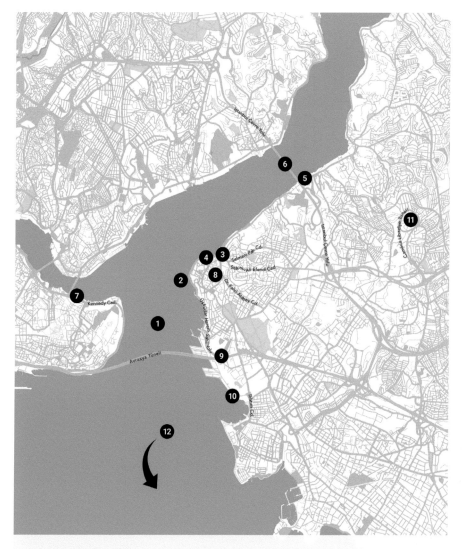

ÜSKÜDAR

1. Bosphorus

2. Maidens Tower

3. Mihrimah Sultan Mosque

4. Shemsi Pasha Mosque

5. Beylerbey Palace

6. 15th July Martyrs' Bridge

7. Uskudar Pier

8. Aziz Mahmud Hudai Mosque

9. Florence Nightingale Museum

10. Haydarpasha Train Station

11. Camlica Mosque

12. Princes Island

Beylerbeyi:

The mini palace

The problem with huge palaces is that they are a little too much for the average person to take in. Once you see your umpteenth sumptuous room, you start to forget what was earlier on the tour.

That is why Beylerbeyi palace is just the right size to truly appreciate the opulence and magnificence of the Sultans. The name itself gives you an indication of what you might find inside; Beylerbeyi means Lord of Lords – a traditional Ottoman title reserved for some of the most senior members of the elite. The area used to be a Byzantine garden and eventually became the home of a Beylerbeyi and then fell out of use.

This perfectly proportioned palace on the Bosphorus was built by the palace-mad Sultan Abdul Aziz. It was originally built to be a guesthouse for visiting royalty.

The first guest was the Empress Eugenie of France who was visiting on her way to the opening of the Suez Canal. Others that have stayed here included the Austro-Hungarian Emperor Franz Joseph, the German Kaiser Wilhelm II and Edward VIII – the King of England and the uncle of the late Queen. This explains the overt European influences in the Palace décor and even the European style toilet.

The crystals are French Baccarat, the carpets are masterpieces from Hereke and the entire building is outfitted in the best material money could buy. The main reception hall is breath-taking with the centrepiece being a large marble swimming pool with gigantic Chinese porcelain vases on each corner. The pool was an innovative way of keeping the interior of the palace cool even during the stifling summer months.

As you walk around and absorb all this splendour in rooms that can hardly contain them, take a moment to consider that this was a palace that the Sultan never meant to live in but just used for guests. No other palace gives you a greater insight into the lavish lifestyles the latter Sultans enjoyed.

Beylerbeyi:

Not Learning from Past Mistakes

On the first occasion an Ottoman flouted the Islamic prohibition on statues, it did not end well for them. The mercurial Grand Vizier found himself dead within days, killed by his own adoring best friend, brother-in-law and Sultan, Suleiman the Magnificent. One would think that such an example would put them off the idea of installing statues forever (if divine retribution was not enough of a warning), but one would be wrong.

Sultan Abdul Aziz was one of the modernising Sultans who did not strictly adhere to the old ways. He decided he would not just install one statue, but many throughout the Beylerbeyi palace. There are statues of his favourite pets, lions, but also of deer's and other wildlife dotted around the parks of Beylerbeyi. However, he went one step further and commissioned a military statue of himself astride a horse. This was too much even for his own mother who promptly had the crate transporting the statue thrown overboard when it arrived from England.

Despite this intervention, it was quietly fished out and installed in Beylerbeyi palace. Just like with Ibrahim Pasha, within a short time, Sultan Abdul Aziz found himself deposed and a prisoner in Topkapı palace. A few days later, he was found dead, and the public explanation given by his courtiers was that he had committed suicide.

A detailed article by the prestigious medical journal, The Lancet, proved that he could not have committed suicide as he was found dead with both his wrists slit. As the eminent forensic physicians pointed out, if the Sultan had slit one wrist to the degree he was said to have, he would not have been physically able to use that wrist to slit the remaining one. Quite apart from the grisly murder of Sultan Abdul Aziz, the installation of statues showed a fatal neglect of lessons from history.

Beylerbeyi:

Even Sultans need to listen to their mother

When the Empress of France visited Constantinople on the way to the grand opening of the Suez Canal, Sultan Abdul Aziz was keen to show her good old fashioned Muslim hospitality. For most people, that would mean taking an interest in what the guest has to say, cooking something special for them and maybe giving them the most comfortable chair. For an Emperor, this meant building a brand-new palace at an enormous cost. Naturally.

When she arrived, Sultan Abdul Aziz was keen to show her around and the Empress was, as expected, amazed by the opulence. They were inspecting the palace arm in arm with their retinues when Sultan Abdul Aziz introduced the Empress to his mother. Instead of polite pleasantries the Valide Sultan, the no-nonsense Pertevinyal, responded by slapping the Empress in the face and dragging her enormous son away by her ear.

How dare he shamelessly hold the arm of an unrelated woman? She had raised him better than this. And so it came to pass that the Sultan, the Caliph, the shadow of God on Earth – begged forgiveness from his mother and promised to behave better in the future.

Beylerbeyi:

Abdul Hamid II prison

After the Young Turks had dethroned the powerful and competent Sultan Abdul Hamid II in a coup, they sent him packing off to Salonica near the edge of the Empire. They knew that he would still be popular if he stayed in Istanbul.

Unfortunately for them, Salonica fell to enemy forces and before he could be captured, Sultan Abdul Hamid II was transported back to Istanbul. This time, he was imprisoned closer to home in the Beylerbey palace.

Sultan Abdul Hamid II, once one of the most powerful men in the world, was kept here restricted to a few rooms. Here he watched from the window no longer able to influence even his own life, let alone that of others. His only companion was one of his wives who chose to remain with him till the end.

He would console himself by undertaking carpentry. Like most Ottoman Sultans, he had to have a "real" job that wasn't just being Sultan. His chosen vocation was woodworking, and he was exceptionally good at it.

As you walk around this Palace turned into a prison, imagine what it must have been like to be surrounded by such opulence but without any freedom. Soon the exquisite porcelain, the sumptuous fabrics and the glittering chandeliers lose their worth when compared to being master of your own destiny, free to move as you wish.

Looking into his bedroom, one can imagine the poignant scene as the elderly Sultan lay dying. All that he had worked to preserve had been lost. The Empire was crumbling, and people were dying or being made refugees in their hundreds of thousands.

As he slipped way, so did the last great hope of the Ottoman family and the Muslim world. Though the institutions of the Sultanate and Caliphate survived for a few more years, the spirit died in this room.

Çamlıca Mosque:

Size is Everything

The Çamlıca hill was the largest of the hills overlooking the ancient city. Recently, the Çamlıca mosque, the largest ever built in Türkiye, was constructed here. While there were protests from those who felt it was a white elephant, the mosque has become an attraction for the area and brought in tourism revenue to a part of the city that traditionally was not included on any itinerary.

The mosque itself is modelled on the architecture of Sinan and there are new features such as day care facilities, improved facilities for female worshippers as well as a small museum.

Four of the balconies are placed deliberately at the height of 107.1 metres commemorating the anniversary of the Battle of Manzikert when the Seljuks defeated the Byzantine Empire. The interior of the dome has 16 divine attributes of Allah, the number being the same as the number of nations founded by Turkish speaking peoples. The dome is also 72 metres high, symbolising the 72 nationalities that were known to live in Istanbul; a reference to the multicultural nature of the city throughout history.

A visit to this mosque is well worth it, with the view it affords of the entire city coming second only to the serenity that one finds within the building itself.

Haydarpaşa:

The Train to Nowhere

Built in the middle of the 1800s, this train station was supposed to be the first stop on the road to Ottoman recovery. Instead, it became a symbol of the disintegration of the Empire. Sultan Abdul Aziz wanted to link his Empire together through a railway system; a system that was being used so effectively by European powers. Haydarpaşa Station would be the first stop for the Hijaz railway and the Berlin to Baghdad Express.

The Berlin to Baghdad Express was supposed to connect the Middle Eastern part of the Empire together. Built by the Germans, it was a geostrategic nightmare for the British and French empires as it provided for German military support to extend across the heart of the Empire and into the Arabian Gulf. However, this line was never completed as WWI intervened and all the main players became occupied with more important things.

The Hijaz railway also started from Haydarpaşa Station. The Hijaz railway was a unique project in that it aimed to be the first serious revolution in the transportation of pilgrims to the Holy cities of Makkah and Madinah since the advent of the steam ship. A personal pet project of Sultan Abdul Hamid II, it was a noble endeavour not only aiming to help ease the transport of pilgrims for the Hajj, but also to demonstrate Ottoman political influence and power across the holy sites. In a mark of the sacred mission of the Hijaz railway, it was paid for by public subscription with funds pouring in from across the world.

Unfortunately, the railway line that was supposed to be a symbol of the unity of the Muslim world, was destroyed by the winds of disunity that were sweeping through it. During World War I in an act of base treachery, the Sharif of Makkah revolted against the embattled Ottomans and began a guerrilla campaign to gain his own kingdom outright.

Aided by military and political agents like Lawrence of Arabia and Gertrude Bell, the Arab tribes began to blow up Ottoman infrastructure as part of their campaign of terrorism and destabilisation. The fact that these acts would destroy infrastructure needed by pilgrims and paid for by the Muslim public mattered little to those who were after their 30 pieces of silver.

It would be at least another 100 years before the first train returned to the Hijaz. It will likely be much longer before any semblance of unity returns.

Princes' Islands:

So Close, Yet so Far

Just a few minutes boat ride out from the shores of Istanbul are the islands known as the Princes' Islands. These are so-called because during Byzantine times, errant princes would be exiled there so that they were cut off from society but not so far away as to be out of sight. Today, they are the location of summer houses of the rich and influential from Turkish society. There are a variety of islands that make up the Princes' Islands including Buyukada, Heybeliada and Burguzada. Because of their locations, they appear almost like a time capsule of the Ottoman Empire with many of the best specimens of homes, avenues and churches still in good repair.

The Aya Yorgi church, atop the highest hill on the Buyukada island, is a beautiful example of what a Byzantine church must have looked like before the conquest. Aya Yorgi is Turkish for St George – the patron saint of England who was ethnically part Palestinian and part Greek from Capadoccia.

In Heybeliada you can find the old home of Ismet Inonu. Ismet Pasha was the second in command to Mustafa Kemal during the War of Independence. He was a brilliant military tactician and engineered the famous victory of the Turkish troops over the Greeks at Inonu. After the battle, Mustafa Kemal insisted that Ismet take the name of this battle as his surname. Ismet Inonu became the leader after Mustafa Kemal and he did well to keep Türkiye out of the second World War till it was all but over. He was not a democrat at heart and was complicit in the army coup of 1960 that ushered decades of coups to come.

The Princes' Islands most conspicuous feature is Maiden's Tower. This building started life as a customs building and defensive position preventing the Muslims from entering the Bosphorus to attack Constantinople by sea. After the conquest it became a lighthouse and eventually even served as a quarantine hospital during the outbreak of plague in the city.

The Maiden's tower is so called because it is believed that a beautiful Greek girl called Hero lived there. When her beloved Leander tried to swim across to see her, he was tossed aside by the waves despite Hero leaving a bright light on to help guide his way. On seeing his body wash up on the shore, Hero threw herself off the tower committing suicide in the Romeo and Juliet style concept of love so common in Western literature

Conclusion

Istanbul has something for everyone. From the Bosphorus with its beautiful vistas to the embarrassment of architectural riches afforded by the old city, every type of appetite and every type of person is catered for. Whether you are an ardent foodie or an intellectual trying to find sustenance for your mind, Istanbul remains one of the top destinations to visit. It was once remarked that if someone was tired of Istanbul, then they are tired of life.

In a Muslim world that is suffering from disunity, dissension and disillusionment with their current reality, Istanbul is a reminder of a once glorious past that is not so distant. It gives hope that with the right leadership, the right mentality and the right vision, they can once again take their place on the world stage.

In the end, my hope is that this book will enable the reader to go beyond being a tourist and experience the city in a way that nourishes the soul too. If we are able to do this, if the buildings and the locations speak to us and inspire us with lessons from the past, then walking through Istanbul won't just be a celebration of the past glories of the Muslim Ummah – it can become a key to a better future.

Bibliography

Aksit, Ilhan. The Mystery of the Ottoman Harem.

Carver, Lord. The National Army Museum Book of the Turkish Front 1914-1918.

Clot, Andre. Suleiman the Magnificent.

Crowley, Roger. Constantinople, The last great siege, 1453.

Dordoncu, Mehmet. The Yildiz Albums of Sultan AbdulHamid II – Mecca to Medina.

Duducu, Jem. The Sultans: The Rise and Fall of the Ottoman Rulers.

Efendi, Turabi. Ottoman Cookery.

Efendi, Abdulmecid. Osmanli Hanedani'ndan Bir Ressam.

Faroqhi, Suraiya. Subjects of the Sultan, Culture and Daily Life in the Ottoman Empire.

Faroqhi, Suraiya. Pilgrims and Sultans, The Hajj under the Ottomans.

Finkel, Caroline. Osman's Dream. The Story of the Ottoman Empire 1300–1923.

Freely, John. Inside the Seraglio, Private lives of the Sultans in Istanbul.

Goodwin, Godfrey. A History of Ottoman Architecture.

Gulersoy, Celik. Dolmabahçe, Palace and its Environs.

Han, Nadine Sultana. The legacy of Sultan AbdulHamid II.

Haslip, Joan. The Sultan, The Life of Sultan AbdulHamid II.

Hopkirk, Peter. On Secret Service East of Constantinople.

Kinross, Patrick. Ataturk, The Rebirth of a Nation.

Mansel, Philip. Constantinople, City of the World's Desire, 1453 – 1924.

McMeekin, Sean. The Berlin-Baghdad Express.

Mihov, Chavdar. The secret power of the Harem.

Minawi, Mostafa. The Ottoman Scramble for Africa.

Miller, Barnette. Beyond the Sublime Porte.

Olcayto, Rory. Sinan, The First Starchitect.

Ortayli, Ilber. Discovering the Ottomans.

Rogers, J and Ward, R. Suleyman the Magnificent.

Stierlin, Henri. Türkiye from the Selcuks to the Ottomans.

Stoneman, Richard. A Traveller's history of Türkiye.

Sumner-Boyd, Hilary and Freely, John. Strolling through Istanbul, The classic guide to the city.

Images

We are grateful for the following for permission to reproduce their images:

Page 20 Portrait of Sultan Ahmed I, The Met, Metmuseum.org

Page 122 Portrait of Sultan Abdul Hamid II, Detail from unknown artist on postcard

Page 230 Exterior of Naval Museum, Adjusted from Viki Picture via Wikimedia

Page 6 Illustration by Halim Erbasi of Inkwell Alchemy

Cover image and Pages 34, 136, 162, 194, 212, 236 Illustrations by House of Places on Etsy

All other images are authors own